How to Think Like
an Entrepreneur
Philip Delves Broughton

MACMILLAN

First published 2016 by Macmillan
an imprint of Pan Macmillan
20 New Wharf Road, London N1 9RR
Associated companies throughout the world
www.panmacmillan.com

ISBN 978-1-4472-9335-4

Copyright © The School of Life 2016

987654321

A CIP catalogue record for this book is
available from the British Library.

Cover design by Marcia Mihotich
Typeset by seagulls.net
Printed and bound by CPI Group (UK) Ltd,
Croydon, CR0 4YY

Visit **www.panmacmillan.com** to
read more about all our books and to
buy them. You will also find features,
author interviews and news of any
author events, and you can sign up for
e-newsletters so that you're always first
to hear about our new releases.

PHILIP DELVES BROUGHTON is the author of two international bestsellers, *Life's a Pitch*, and *What They Teach You at Harvard Business School*. He grew up in England, received his BA in Classics from Oxford and his MBA from Harvard Business School. He spent ten years as a reporter and foreign correspondent for the *Daily Telegraph* and now writes regularly for the *Financial Times* and the *Wall Street Journal*. An edited collection of his work for the *FT* was published as *Management Matters: From the Humdrum to the Big Decisions*. He also collaborates with the Kauffman Foundation for Entrepreneurship and Education in the area of research and policy.

THE SCHOOL OF LIFE is dedicated to exploring life's big questions: *How do we find fulfilling work? Can we ever understand our past? Why are relationships so hard to master? If we could change the world, should we?* Based in London, with campuses around the globe, The School of Life offers classes, therapies, books and other tools to help you create a more satisfying life. We don't have all the answers but we will direct you towards a variety of ideas from the humanities – from philosophy to literature, psychology to the visual arts – guaranteed to stimulate, provoke, nourish and console.

By the same author:

Life's a Pitch

What They Teach You at Harvard Business School

Management Matters: From the Humdrum to the Big Decisions

To Hugo and Augie

Contents

Introduction

I.

Most new businesses fail. Most entrepreneurs fail. Even those who succeed suffer through the process. The jaunty, sunny character who first seizes upon an idea and decides to bring it to market soon becomes grizzled by experience, by the violence of the competition, the disdain of investors, the treachery of employees.

Paul Graham, the founder of Y Combinator, one of the more successful of Silicon Valley's entrepreneurial incubator programmes, says the underlying reason most start-ups fail is that they become demoralized. Yet another investor turns them down. Yet another client loses interest. Yet *another* cheque gets bounced by the stiffs at the bank. Each individual adversity could be dealt with if morale was still high. But once it's gone, so goes hope. 'If you can just avoid dying,' Graham says, 'you get rich.'[1]

Yet now more than ever, the life of the entrepreneur is celebrated and desired. Incubators and accelerators from Palo Alto to Brooklyn, from East London to Berlin are humming with ambitious entrepreneurs, confident that they can beat the daunting odds. You could spend every week of the year at a conference where successful entrepreneurs roll onstage in their vintage Adidas and designer jeans to talk of the importance of fast failure and pivoting out of disaster.

Given how many presentations Sir Richard Branson seems to make before audiences of adoring entrepreneurs, it is a miracle he has time to run his business.

The economist Daniel Kahneman would say that the phenomenon of the start-up hub, the busy cafes of Hoxton Square in London or University Avenue in Palo Alto, lead to an acute case of WYSIATI – What You See Is All There Is. If you are surrounded by others doing the same thing as you, a few successfully but all with a good degree of swagger, you tend to ignore the risks of your undertaking. Your head swims with stories of billion dollar 'exits', of acquisitions by technology giants, and before you know it you don't worry about buying an expensive coffee with an expensive credit card for a meeting that may go nowhere. All those TED talks you watch about risk-taking and abundance, about avoiding a life of quiet desperation and embarking on that entrepreneurial adventure, are a contagious form of ignorance.

Kahneman writes:

> The emotional, cognitive and social factors that support exaggerated optimism are a heady brew, which sometimes lead people to take risks that they would avoid if they knew the odds. There is no evidence that risk takers in the economic domain have an unusual appetite for gambles on high stakes; they are merely less aware of risks than more timid people are.

The optimism of entrepreneurs, he says, is 'widespread, stubborn and costly'.[2]

If there was any honesty among those who teach and promote entrepreneurship, they would tear down the inspiring quotes pasted up on their office walls and replace them with pictures of people being rejected at cashpoints. They would hand out T-shirts saying: 'You built a food-delivery app to change the world – and all you got was this lousy eviction notice.' That would be more consistent with the facts of entrepreneurial risk-taking.

But they don't because there are countervailing forces at work. There is the profound psychological need which entrepreneurship can satisfy. To succeed as an entrepreneur is a form of heroic achievement in any economy, but particularly a vigorous market economy. To become a multibillionaire through your own endeavour affords you fawning respect, invitations to state dinners, honorary doctorates, Hollywood biopics.

Entrepreneurship offers a way out of corporate life, out of a system of task-and-reward allocation run by others, to one run by you. You get to decide how to work, what to work on, and how to divide the rewards. If you would rather wear your skivvies instead of a suit, forego all meetings and work via Skype from the beach, you can – assuming your investors and employees still trust you to make your business fly. At the very least, when you find yourself hauled out of bed early on a weekend morning, or taking that last, grey flight home on a Friday night, you can know you are doing it for yourself rather than at the whim of another.

But entrepreneurship also allows individuals a shot at the even deeper pleasure of doing work that they cannot do while working for others. It provides a way to innovate, to challenge whatever currently prevails and to let your originality flourish.

Barbecue fuels the optimism of East London's start-up scene.

If you are a medical researcher and you know a new drug could help thousands of people, but not enough to make commercial sense for the pharmaceutical company you work for, entrepreneurship offers you a path. If you are a chef chafing on the line, yearning to create dishes which exist only in your imagination, finding investors and opening your own restaurant is a way to turn that yearning into action. If you are a young musician struggling to be heard, you can make your own recordings and distribute them yourself. If you are an ambitious politician, an African American, say, who has served only two years in the US Senate but think you have a long-shot at the White House, it takes entrepreneurial thinking to orchestrate a successful campaign.

Entrepreneurship is a powerful means of arranging life to enable one's fulfilment, and it is this ineffable opportunity which colours people's view of its risks. Business is often wrongly seen as a set of rational processes. Entrepreneurship gives emotion its proper place.

And before we plunge in, let me offer one more kink in our understanding of entrepreneurial thinking. When Daniel Kahneman wrote that optimism was dangerous for entrepreneurs, he added that it was most dangerous when it came to making the decision to launch a venture. Once the venture was underway, optimists tended to do better than pessimists: 'Confidence in their future success sustains a positive mood that helps them obtain resources from others, raise the morale of their employees, and enhance the prospects of prevailing. When action is needed, optimism, even of the mildly delusional variety, may be a good thing.'[3]

A few years ago, an old friend received millions of dollars of venture-capital investment in his new company, which was barely a few weeks old. He was frazzled with anxiety and excitement. As we sat in his car after dinner, he could barely stay still, his fingers drumming the steering wheel, his thoughts racing out ahead of him. He held out his palm, pointed at it and said in an excited whisper: 'I feel like I'm holding a tiny dragon. All I have to do is not fuck it up.'

To think like an entrepreneur is to journey through this mazy terrain between optimism and despair: optimism engendered by the thrill of self-actualization which occurs when you start and manage a successful enterprise; and despair at the difficulties which this entails and the corpses which litter your path. It is a journey many people are eager to travel and for which this book is intended as a guide.

2.

The most widely accepted modern definition of entrepreneurship was coined by Howard Stevenson, a professor at Harvard Business School. It states that 'Entrepreneurship is the pursuit of opportunity without regard to resources currently controlled.' The appeal of this definition is as much in what it leaves out as in what it contains. It does not contain the word 'risk' because Stevenson felt that most entrepreneurs do not see themselves as risk-junkies. They are willing to take the risks necessary to achieve their often difficult goals, but they abhor pointless risk. Gustave Flaubert advised that artists should be 'regular and orderly in your life like a bourgeois, so that you may be violent and original in your work'. He might just as well have been advising entrepreneurs.

Stevenson's definition also does not limit the practice of entrepreneurship to those who start and grow their own company, because he believed that you do not have to start and grow a company to behave in an entrepreneurial fashion. A corporate manager who finds a novel way to persuade and organize others to create a new product is by Stevenson's definition practising a kind of entrepreneurship, pursuing opportunity without regard to the resources currently under her control. An artist who explores untested media and collaborations to bring a concept to life is doing the same. An entrepreneur is a person who resists ever feeling stuck because they don't currently have what it takes to pursue a dream or opportunity. An entrepreneur finds a way to resist the easy default settings of modern life, to pursue a path that is their own.

When Barack Obama considered running for the presidency in 2008, he had few of the necessary resources, only an accumulation of encouraging evidence. As he toured America promoting his book *The Audacity of Hope*, crowds fizzed with excitement. Old warhorses of the Democratic Party would come to watch him speak, and go away shaking their heads in awe, comparing him to Bobby Kennedy.[4] He had been thinking of himself as a leader from the moment he arrived at Harvard Law School and realized that he was comfortable leading within this future political elite. Now his aides began telling him that he needed to prepare, just in case a 'perfect storm' of events gave him a shot at victory. He was bored of being a mere senator, bored of the sausage-factory of legislation, and imagined he could be more effective as the country's top political executive. He had developed such a knack for fundraising from wealthy Democrats that he was nicknamed 'Money'. His entrepreneurial mind was awhirr.

Some advised him it was too early, just two years since he had been elected to the senate. Others said that the window of opportunity to run for president opened and shut quickly. He would be foolish not to leap through. He was young and considered non-partisan. But he lacked experience and the support of the Democratic Party's core. He was the hot thing now, but could he cope with the criticism inevitable in a campaign? There was the fact of his being African American. His wife, Michelle, was nervous about the effect on their family, their two young daughters. A few days before he announced his candidacy, his eventual campaign manager, David Axelrod, told him: 'I think you have ambition, but not that kind of pathological drive' he would need to win.[5]

He spent Christmas discussing the decision with his family, then called his advisors: he was in. Like any good entrepreneur, he was chasing his opportunity, weighing his chances and making lists. This was not an entrepreneurial decision in a business sense, but it met Stevenson's criteria. At the moment Obama decided to pursue the opportunity of the White House, he controlled few of the resources he would need, but trusted he would acquire them.

This is not a book to help you negotiate a term sheet or value a seed-round for a new enterprise. Nor will it lay out the tactics for forcing a new project through layers of corporate bureaucracy. But it will describe the ways in which you will need to think as you decide first whether to be an entrepreneur, then what ideas to pursue and how to survive the inevitable challenges.

3.

Economists can be timid souls, leery of steeping outside their austere mathematical cages. Not so the American Edmund Phelps, who was

A political entrepreneur contemplating the resources currently under his control.

awarded the Nobel Prize in economics in 2006. Phelps believes that there is a strong link between economies which thrive and grow and societies which give individuals the freedoms to flourish. He has studied the most dynamic economies in recent history, Britain in the 1820s, France in the Roaring 1920s and America in the 1960s, and concluded that:

> Understanding the modern economies must start with a modern notion: original ideas born of creativity and grounded on the uniqueness of each person's private knowledge, information, and imagination. The modern economies were driven by the new ideas of the whole roster of business people mostly unsung: idea men, entrepreneurs, marketers and pioneering end-users.[6]

Societies during these periods of economic dynamism were not just modern economically, but also socially. Prejudices were shed, social freedoms expanded and more people allowed to participate in political, economic and cultural life. The more people in a society who are happy to be part of it and encouraged to be themselves and to thrive, the more dynamic that society's economy will be. It can be disconcerting for members of the old order. Societies will often use the excuse of needing to maintain social order to resist what Phelps describes as 'the topsy-turvy of creation, the frenzy of development, and painful closings when the new things fail to take hold'. But these have been the conditions for the most dynamic growth. These are the conditions in which entrepreneurs have historically done well. Without the seething mass of individuals freed to use their knowledge and talents to propel an economy forward, it will stagnate.

A traditional economy, in Phelps's distinction, produces 'known, specified goods', whereas a modern economy dreams of what it might produce and tries to turn those dreams into reality. That modern economy is where thinking entrepreneurs can run riot, expressing themselves, bending the arc of their own lives and the societies around them.

Another way to think about this is to see modern capitalist societies being yanked tight by two contradictory powers, the corporatist and the individual. Corporatism favours large interest groups, companies, political parties, unions and religions, and the achievement of social consensus. The corporatist goal is not growth or mobility but harmony, with everyone quite happy where they are. The corporatists' greatest fear is volatility, booms and busts in the economy and social unrest.

Ambitious individuals are more interested in opportunity and change. They want to see people rise and fall on their merits. They don't want consensus if it is just aspic poured over the existing social order to preserve its shape. They would much prefer turbulence if it provides a path to growth and improvement.

These are not left–right political distinctions. There are corporatists and individualists on both sides. The prim conservative, who sees even the mildest grunt from the economic class directly beneath as a sign of imminent revolution, is as much a corporatist as the union boss who insists his workers' rights be guaranteed even when his employer has to compete with lower-wage rivals around the world. Both find comfort in being part of a much larger social group, and will wage war to protect their position.

The expansion of individual freedom and entrepreneurial activity occur simultaneously.

The most important decisions for modern economies, then, revolve around the balance between satisfying the corporatists and the individualists, between those wanting to preserve what exists and divide it up so no one feels too hard done by, and those who want more. Technology has only complicated this balance, as it has created millions of opportunities for self-employment but without the social protections embedded in traditional jobs. Corporatists demand to know if the Uber driver is a contractor or an employee. Individualists say it scarcely matters, provided drivers are happy with the work. When they succeed, entrepreneurs flout this kind of needling discussion as they get on with their economic business.

I mention all of this to explain why thinking like an entrepreneur can so often feel uncomfortable. People with much to protect are not always inclined to support those agitating for change.

Yet to think like an entrepreneur is to be modern. To want change, to search for opportunity and then be willing to pursue it. Those three steps of want, search and pursuit can put the entrepreneurially minded at odds with those around them. Bringing change to an established market, introducing a novel political idea, adopting a new creative technique or changing the expectations of an audience can require a degree of force. Even the nicest entrepreneur must sometimes apply the Chinese burn to achieve the novelty she desires. Their demanding nature can make entrepreneurs easy targets for criticism. Until, of course, they are proved correct, and suddenly they are glorious rebels, the heroes of our capitalist age.

4.

In the early 1990s, a multibillionaire from Kansas City named Ewing Kauffman was looking to establish a foundation, but struggling to find a purpose. He hired advisors and sent them out to study the work of other great American foundations, named after Ford, Rockefeller and Carnegie, which focused on public health, education and world peace. After much consideration, Kauffman decided that his foundation should address the two factors which he felt had transformed his own life: education and entrepreneurship. He had grown up poor and socially disadvantaged. But thanks to a sound education and the opportunity to create his own business he had become one of the most influential men in the American Midwest. He built a pharmaceuticals business named Marion Labs, which he sold for several billion dollars, and owned the Kansas City Royals baseball team. Dozens of his employees became millionaires and they in turn had changed the face of their city, investing in more businesses and donating to schools, hospitals and cultural institutions.

The central question for Kauffman's foundation became this: how can one expose more people to the transformational opportunities of entrepreneurship? It is a question that requires consideration of regulations and taxation, the availability of credit and education, intellectual property rights and social mobility. But it also requires a basic understanding of people, of those willing to assume an entrepreneurial challenge, and those not. It forces us to ask what in the character of an entrepreneur is born, and what is made, what is nature and what nurture. We need to think about the risks entrepreneurs must manage, and whether these should be mitigated to encourage more people to become entrepreneurs, or accentuated to haze out the likely failures sooner rather than later. We need to work hard to understand what it means to think and act like an entrepreneur, because the word contains multitudes.

I. The Entrepreneurial Mind

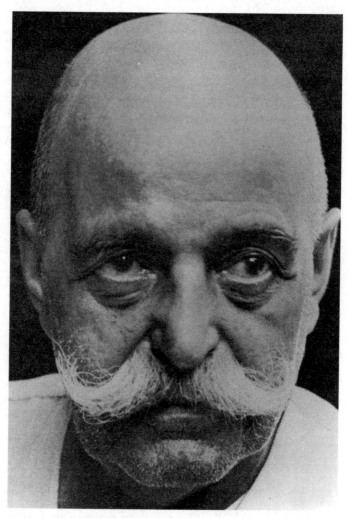

George Gurdjieff. Entrepreneur, mystic, survivor.

1. The Material Question

In April 1924, George Gurdjieff, the Armenian-born founder of the Institute for the Harmonious Development of Man, visited New York to raise money for his new enterprise. Over a dessert of watermelon at the home of a supporter, he was asked how he planned to cover his operation's expenses. Gurdjieff, a striking-looking man with a bald head and luscious, handlebar moustache, replied that he would give a full and honest answer since he was 'breathing this air saturated with the vibrations of people who sow and reap dollars in a masterly fashion', and 'like a thoroughbred hunting dog' was 'on the scent of certain and good game'.[1]

When Gurdjieff was a child, he told his rapt audience, his father told him stories about a lame carpenter named Mustafa who could make anything from wood, even a flying armchair. These stories had nurtured a desire in Gurdjieff always 'to be making something new'. His first teacher never let him practise the same craft for long. The moment he became familiar with one and began to like it, his teacher moved him on to the next. 'As I understood much later, his aim was not that I should learn all sorts of crafts but should develop in myself the ability to surmount the difficulties presented by any kind of new work,' Gurdjieff said. 'As a result I acquired, even if only automatically, abilities of both a theoretical and practical nature for carrying on various manual and commercial occupations. My comprehension also was gradually increased as my horizon widened in various fields of knowledge.'

His mind was not cluttered with the debris of a formal education. Rather, he had a way of thinking and addressing the world which allowed him throughout his life to earn 'despicable and maleficent money for unavoidable needs'.

In 1899, he was travelling by train through modern Turkmenistan, en route to a meeting of a 'Community of Truth Seekers', when he met a Mme Vitvitskaia, a fellow truth-seeker. They made a wager that by a specific date Gurdjieff had to make a certain sum of money.

Gurdjieff considered the matter and decided to disembark in Ashkhabad, a young town, affluent but still uncultivated. Its residents, mostly retired government officials, were suckers for new merchandise. Tradesmen would flock here to sell new goods they could not sell elsewhere, knowing that the locals would buy anything if they were convinced it was modern and sophisticated. Consequently, many households in town were swamped with broken gizmos. Gurdjieff found a basic workshop opening onto the street, equipped it with a few simple tools and announced himself with a sign:

AMERICAN TRAVELLING WORKSHOP
HERE FOR A VERY SHORT TIME
MAKES, ALTERS AND REPAIRS EVERYTHING

The next day, the Ashkhabadians began lining up with machines Gurdjieff never imagined existed: one for removing grey hairs, another for stoning cherries, a special iron for ironing wigs. It was customary in this part of the Russian empire never to part with anything once acquired, so as well as broken novelties, the people of Ashkhabad also had troves of old possessions, from their grandparents' spectacles to rusting medals. When they found a man who would repair everything, they flocked to him.

Gurdjieff was unscrupulous. When a 'rich, fat Armenian puffing and bathed in perspiration' brought him a sewing machine and complained it was broken, Gurdjieff noticed that all it took to make it work was to press a lever on the side. But rather than telling his customer this, he said it would require three days' work and several replacement parts. He skinned a local regimental commander who sent him a consignment of new typewriters. The commander thought they were faulty, when in fact all they needed was their spools of ribbon rewound. Gurdjieff again pretended the fix would be complicated and was paid accordingly. He kept pulling the same tricks in town after town, dealing in everything from old corsets to artificial flowers, and not only won the wager but accumulated a considerable fortune in the process. From this, he moved on to buying and selling oil, railways and antique rugs, until World War I interrupted his moneymaking.

This experience of making do against the odds, of answering what he called 'the material question' whenever it presented itself, fortified him. Every entrepreneur must do the same, address reality and find a way to survive and make money during the uncertain pursuit of a goal. Answering the question successfully when it was posed made Gurdjieff fearless and fast-moving when he travelled through the Caucasus, through fighting between the Bolshevik and White Russian armies. It helped him support members of his family

If you can find your customers' pain and heal it, how you do it and how much you charge will scarcely matter.

whose lives were upended by war and revolution and who arrived on his doorstep in Tiflis, modern Tblisi, 'skeletons of people, with only their burning eyes alive, clad in rags and tatters, their bare feet covered with wounds and sores'. It propelled him to France where in 1922 he set up his institute to teach self-development. Despite not speaking a word of French, he managed to rebuild his fortunes through ceaseless work.

In the last sections of Gurdjieff's reflection on the 'material question' he comes across more as a charlatan than a mystic, a man on a constant wheel of financial ambition, overextension and frantic dealing to escape his debts so he can finally live a 'higher' life free of material want. There was no happy ending. The material question overwhelmed him. The freedom he sought proved elusive.

2. Cognitive Complexity

A great deal of nonsense is written about the psychology of entrepreneurs. They are said to have the mindsets of juvenile delinquents, or to be engaged in dark, psychological rivalries with their fathers. They are described as risk addicts and control freaks, intuitive and rigorous, charismatic, evangelical, terrified of insignificance, with the creativity of Michelangelo, the madness of Van Gogh and the military discipline of Rommel.[2] The list of traits goes on into irrelevance, because the traits we find in successful entrepreneurs we find in successful people in all kinds of fields. It may be that the only common psychological thread among entrepreneurs, from the thrifty dry-goods merchant to the razzle-dazzle hedge-fund baron, is that they choose to be entrepreneurs.

That said, there are, I believe, two habits of mind worth examining. The first is cognitive complexity, or the ability to see relationships between very different fields of knowledge. And the second is greed, or ambition if you are squeamish.

Gurdjieff might not seem the most obvious example of entrepreneurial thought and action, but his account of dealing with the 'material question' reveals a high degree of cognitive complexity. Cognitive complexity is different from raw intelligence. It reveals itself in a tolerance of new ideas, in curiosity about experiences which challenge you. Those who possess it are empathetic to people very different from themselves, and have the imagination to understand conflicting points of view. They venture eagerly and playfully into the unknown and are thus more likely to discover new things than those who set out in fear. They trust that the world will take care of them.

The historian J. Rogers Hollingsworth sought to examine the roots of cognitive complexity in several hundred scientists who had won major scientific prizes, such as the Nobel. He found two consistent patterns in their lives. The first was that many had internalized multiple cultures. This means more than visiting a few countries on holiday. Internalization requires immersing oneself so deeply in a different culture that one can understand it and inhabit it intuitively.[3]

In 1988, the Nobel Prize in physiology or medicine was won by Gertrude Elion, George Hitchings and Sir James Black. Elion's parents had emigrated to New York, her father from Lithuania, her mother from a part of Russia now in Poland. Her family was Jewish and devout, and she grew up studying religion and speaking both Yiddish and English. When she decided as a young girl to become a scientist, she knowingly entered a world dominated by men. The experience of being Jewish, American and a woman in a male-dominated profession, Hollingsworth suggested, contributed to the complexity of her thinking. James Black also assumed multiple identities growing up. His father was a mining engineer and colliery manager, a member of the upper-middle class. But Black went to school in Lanarkshire, Scotland, with the children of miners and later used that experience of navigating between two worlds, that of the miners and the managers they loathed, to shuttle confidently between different scientific fields.

Another way to learn another culture is to be marginalized, to be forced into new and awkward social positions. Hollingsworth found among his scientists men and women who because of their intelligence as children had been forced into classes with much older peers. They sacrificed friendships and normal socialization for the sake of their academic progress. The evolutionary biologist E. O. Wilson suffered a more extreme form of marginalization. He was born in Birmingham, Alabama, but after his parents divorced when he was seven, his alcoholic father passed him around from the homes of family and strangers to boarding houses. In every town he found himself Wilson would head for the edges, for the swamps, rivers and woods. 'Animals and plants I could count on; human relationships were more difficult.'

Wilson attended more than a dozen schools, and when he finally graduated from high school, his father killed himself. 'Strong father, weak son,' Wilson wrote in his memoir, *Naturalist*, 'weak father, strong son; either way, pain drives the son up or down in life.'[4] It drove him up, to study his way to a professorship at Harvard, the National Medal of Science and two Pulitzer Prizes for his writing. But it was the experience of being pushed to the borders between cultures, constantly being both inside and outside different worlds, which formed an unusually complex, insightful mind. In his most famous book, *Consilience: The Unity of Knowledge*,[5] he argued that the most powerful conclusions were to be reached by gluing back together all the knowledge which had been fragmented over the past two centuries. We lose when we overspecialize and win when we can make connections between diverse fields.

The second pattern Hollingsworth noticed in the lives of prizewinning scientists were 'mentally intensive avocations'. These

Isolation and marginalization forge fresh perspectives.

avocations were usually quite apart from science, but pursued with equal passion. Many of the scientists were serious musicians, painters or writers. Einstein often credited his theory of relativity to intuition nourished by music. 'For many scientists,' wrote Hollingsworth, 'their activities as an artist, painter, musician, poet, etc., enhanced their skills in pattern formation and pattern recognition, skills that they could transfer back and forth between science and art. It was part of their ability to understand reality in more than one way.'[6] Scientists who can express themselves in both equations and understandable prose are thought to have a deeper understanding of their own work. That pivoting between fields of vision and perspectives, that immersion in multiple worlds, benefits entrepreneurs as it does scientists. Entrepreneurs must also be many things: thinkers and doers, artists and scientists, lone decision-makers and dependable team-builders.

3. Wanting It

In 2011, when Bill Gates visited the University of Washington, a student asked him how she could become as rich as he was. Gates said he never started out with the goal of being super-rich. 'Most people who have done well have just found something they're nuts about doing. Then they figure out a system to hire their friends to do it with them. If it's an area of great impact then sometimes you get financial independence.' Money above a certain level, he said, became yet another responsibility. 'I can understand about having millions of dollars. There's meaningful freedom that comes with that, but once you get much beyond that, I have to tell you, it's the same hamburger.'[7]

Successful entrepreneurs can have wildly different attitudes to money. Some love to brandish it, to show off with jets and homes around the world. Richard Branson, the founder of Virgin, revels in showing off Necker, his private Caribbean island. Roman Abramovich, who made his fortune by scooping up cheap energy assets following the collapse of the Soviet Union, glowers from the owner's box at Chelsea Football Club. Others go in the opposite direction and seem to minimize money's importance, as if the mission of their work is far more important than its financial rewards. Mark Zuckerberg, the founder of Facebook, still wears the same uniform of T-shirt and jeans he wore as a student at Harvard, despite earning some $30 billion in the decade after he dropped out. Great fortunes may not have been these entrepreneurs' only goal, but they were certainly a natural consequence of meeting Gates's entrepreneurial requirement of 'doing something they're nuts about' in an area of great impact.

Money can be a wonderful reward for entrepreneurs. But it's not the only one. And to think like an entrepreneur, you need to know what it is you value most and to stick to it whatever distractions come your way.

For entrepreneurs who succeed, a common challenge is deciding whether they wish to be 'rich or king'. It is rare to be both, because the skills it takes to launch a company and the skills it takes to run a company once it has achieved significant scale are very different. Founders are often bought out along the way, or shoved aside by investors, in favour of more experienced executives. If your primary goal is to be rich, losing control scarcely matters if you are paid handsomely for your work. But if your goal was to build and manage a growing enterprise, then losing control can be traumatic, no matter the size of your pay-off. Post-entrepreneurial life can seem pretty empty, even with a large cheque.

Similarly, if you are an entrepreneur within a large organization, you may have to decide if you want to own the consequences of your successful change, or simply sit back with a promotion and the glory. Either way, you will have to decide what it is you became an entrepreneur for, to acquire wealth and influence and step back for growth's sake, or to be king over a smaller domain. What itch does your entrepreneurship need to scratch?

Riccardo Tisci, the creative director of Givenchy, grew up in Taranto, a coastal city in the heel of Italy. He was the youngest of nine children, and when he was six years old, his father died of a heart attack. At school in the 1980s, his tastes ran to English bands like The Cure and Siouxsie and the Banshees, and by the time he was seventeen, he and his mother agreed he had to leave. 'I knew if I stayed there, I would be poor forever,' he said.[8] So off he went to London, where he worked as a cleaner and then as an assistant to the designer Antonio Berardi, before winning a place at Central Saint Martin's fashion school on a government grant. For his graduation show, he wanted a particular model, Mariacarla Boscono, to wear his clothes. Her agent declined, but Tisci kept coming, asking repeatedly in different ways until eventually Boscono relented. 'What hit me most was that he could not stop,' she said. 'He was obsessed almost. Like Van Gogh. Those psycho artists.'[9]

By the time he was thirty-one, Tisci was in charge of Givenchy and within ten years had made it the hottest label in fashion, favoured by music and movie stars, athletes and the merely very rich. He now flitted between his homes in Paris and New York, holidays in Rio and Ibiza, his fear of being poor relegated to his subconscious.

Greed can take many forms, not all of them monstrous. Tisci was greedy for escape from the suffocating lack of opportunity in southern Italy. This turned into greed for success in the hypercompetitive world of fashion, and is now greed for friendships and ever more dazzling shows. Though an employee of Givenchy, he displays all the novelty-seeking appetites of an entrepreneur.

During the 1970s, the oil tycoon John Paul Getty wrote a series of essays titled *How to Be Rich* for *Playboy* magazine. The vigorous young readers of *Playboy*, he believed, represented the future of American business much more than the more sedate readers of

Fortune or *Time*. In one of these essays, he described four kinds of people. The first are those who work for themselves and never want to be employed by anyone. They value their independence far above the security of employment. The second group join businesses and do tremendously well, reaching the most senior positions and pulling in the largest salaries and bonuses. The third group also work for others, and do so conscientiously but unspectacularly. The final group work for others but 'have the same attitude toward their employers that postal clerks have toward the Post Office Department'. They are not motivated to produce a profit for their employer, which does not demand one. (The US postal service is an independent agency of the federal government.) They may be intelligent and competent, but provided they receive their salaries have no interest in improving the productivity or profits of their employer.

Getty argued that what the first two groups possessed and the last two groups lacked was 'the Millionaire Mentality', which is 'cost-conscious and profit-minded'. The man with a Millionaire Mentality is not a 'penny-pincher and money-grubber' but he knows the value of a dollar and cares about it. He is also, in the most successful cases, a strident individual, impatient with needless convention. 'He can wear a green toga instead of a gray-flannel suit, drink yak's milk rather than Martinis, drive a Kibitka instead of a Cadillac and vote the straight Vegetarian Ticket – and none of it will make the slightest difference. Ability and achievement are bona fides no one dares question, not matter how unconventional the man who presents them.'

Getty's father, who started building the family fortune, adhered to a maxim of Sir Francis Bacon: 'No man's fortune can be an end worthy of his being.' He considered money the result of success in business, but thought it should be used not only for consumption, for furs and caviar, but to reinvest in new opportunities, to create jobs and incite social progress.

The entrepreneur should be greedy for success, because with success all kinds of new opportunities present themselves. An independent spirit and an appetite for success, of which money can be a significant marker, is what sets the flywheel of entrepreneurial achievement in motion. Such greed is nothing to be ashamed of.

4. Age vs Experience

Contemporary entrepreneurship can seem like the realm of the young. In the spring of 2013, the British press was dazzled by Nick D'Aloisio, who had created a software application to summarize text and sold it to Yahoo! for $30 million. He was seventeen, one of the youngest self-made millionaires in history. Mark Zuckerberg started Facebook when he was twenty. By the time his company went public four days after his twenty-eighth birthday, he was worth well over $20 billion.

Michael Moritz, a Welsh venture capitalist who made his name investing in companies like Amazon and Google, once said the greatest thrill of his job was working with entrepreneurs in their mid twenties, who 'see no boundaries, see no limits, see no obstacle that they can't hurdle'.[10] He boasted of investing in a company whose three founders had a collective age of sixty-four. He cited the examples of Steve Jobs of Apple, Bill Gates of Microsoft, Larry Ellison of Oracle and Michael Dell of Dell Computers, sensational entrepreneurs who had started their businesses in their late teens or early twenties. There was something magical about that age, he said, when entrepreneurs have great passion and 'they don't have distractions like families and children and other things that get in the way of business'. Moritz was speaking to an audience at a conference in Silicon Valley, and Eric Schmidt, then CEO of

Google, interrupted to say that the pertinent issue was not age, but cost. Venture capitalists like to invest in the young because, all else being equal, they are cheap. 'What you want is the people who are very low paid, working themselves to death, and all the right things happen,' said Schmidt. Moritz tried a joke: 'You think it should be roughly $1,000 per year or $2,000 per year of age?' 'Don't dig yourself a deeper hole,' said Schmidt.

Research into the motivations and backgrounds of American entrepreneurs published in 2013 found that the average age at which they started their first companies was forty. Nearly 70 per cent were married at the time, and nearly 60 per cent had at least one child.[11] Not exactly Moritz's ideal. The discrepancy might be explained by the fact that entrepreneurs and venture capitalists choose each other. VCs take a portfolio approach to investing. They expect nine out of ten of their investments to fail, and to be covered by one gigantic hit. One Google pays for a lot of busts. They tease out their funds accordingly, investing as little as they can to receive as much as they can, throwing in some 'in-kind' perks like networking and introductions in return for even more equity. They love the young and the hungry.

Older entrepreneurs are less willing to be included in a portfolio where the expectations of success are so low. They bring experience and industry know-how and perhaps their own capital. They likely have more to lose than an entrepreneur in his early twenties. Not only do the VCs have less need for them, they have less need for the VCs.

But rather than thinking about a particular age at which it is best to become an entrepreneur, it is more useful to identify the moment when you have the energy and competence required to start your enterprise in balance.

Energy is the easy part to measure. As we become older, our capacity to stay up late, to put in long hours, to slug back burnt coffee straight from the pot and pop glucose supplements deep into the night, diminishes. Also, the intensity of our commitments outside work tends to increase. We build relationships, acquire families and financial obligations. If all we needed when we were twenty-one was some nearly clean clothes and enough money for the rent and a bowl of noodles, by the time we are lurching into middle age the bills tend to have multiplied along with the claims on our time. Our nights and weekends are now shared by others. The energy we have left over to start a business is diminished.

Competence is more complicated. There is straightforward technical competence, knowledge of computer programming, for example, which can be acquired by teenagers, who can create an application and sell it for millions. But that is different from building a business. For that, different kinds of competence are required. First you need credibility to attract investors and employees to your idea. Then you might need managerial experience to build your organization. If you are opening a restaurant, you need to know about food preparation, if it's a limousine service, about the occupational licensing and insurance rules governing your industry. The economist Gary Becker applied the term 'human capital' to this field, the sum total of our education, training, health and subtler qualities emerging from experience. The fact that we tend to improve our human capital over time explains why older people are paid more than younger people in most organizations. The old are rewarded for all the training and experience they have acquired, while the young are charged for receiving it.

A simple field in which to understand the balance between competence and energy is sports. In a sport like soccer, players can burst on to the professional scene in their late teens, but tend to retire by their mid thirties. They start playing the full ninety minutes of every game, brimful of energy and speed, and end as guileful passers and tacklers, coming off the bench to affect the last twenty minutes of a game. In tennis, Roger Federer's later years are so admired because he plays with all the cunning of experience, while retaining the energy of youth. This rare feat has kept him at the top of his sport for an unusually long time.

In every industry there are different dynamics at play. It is rare to see architects getting serious projects much before they turn fifty. The people who pay for buildings like to see a few grey hairs in the people they commission. Unlike a software application, you cannot iterate endlessly and cheaply with a building. Once it starts going up, the costs to change it might sink you.

5. The Old Man and the Fish

When Frank Gehry graduated from the architecture school at the University of Southern California, he applied for a job with Richard Neutra, Los Angeles's reigning modernist. Neutra was impressed by the twenty-five-year-old Gehry and offered him a post. But when Gehry asked about the salary, Neutra told him that he would have to pay for the privilege of working alongside him. Gehry was offended and turned down the opportunity.[12] He had chosen to live and work in Los Angeles because it was a 'city free of the burdens of history', not so he could run up debts as an intern.

He sought the company of artists and architects, but found himself marginalized by both. The architects tried to belittle him by calling him an 'artist', while the artists called him a 'plumber'.[13] But Gehry drew his energy from straddling these worlds.

> There was a powerful, powerful energy I was getting from this [art] scene that I wasn't getting from the architecture world. What attracted me to them is that they worked intuitively. They would do what they wanted and take the consequences. Their work was more direct and in such contrast to what I was doing in architecture, which was so rigid. You have to deal with safety issues – fireproofing, sprinklers, handrails for stairways, things like that. You go through training that

The oldest life forms inspire the newest forms of creativity – provided you can make the connections.

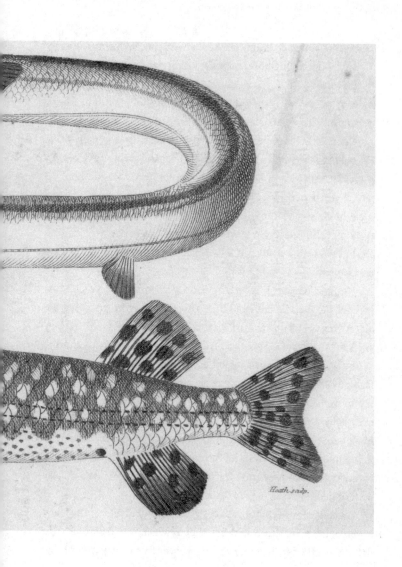

Heath sculp.

teaches you to do things in a very careful way, following codes and budgets. But those constraints didn't speak to aesthetics.[14]

As with the Nobel Prize winners studied by Hollingsworth, Gehry was moving between fields, marginalized and keenly observant.

Gehry built his reputation within his profession over many years. He battled between doing work for money and trying to develop a personal aesthetic. As he tried to answer the 'material question', he flirted with bankruptcy. He built objects and buildings out of unusual materials: plywood, cardboard and corrugated metal. It was not until 1997 that the Bilbao Guggenheim opened and he became famous around the world. And even the idea for that came from the unlikeliest source.

He had long been searching for a way to decorate a building without the usual, traditional decorations. And as he pondered the oldest kinds of life forms, he began to draw fish. He noticed how they appeared to be moving even when they were still, their scales glinting in the water. His first fish-inspired design was a thirty-seven-foot fashion catwalk for a show in Italy in 1985. As he sought to represent the movement and grace of a fish, he stripped down his ideas and eventually turned to computers to design the swoops and curves he imagined. Though he knew little about computers, there were people in his studio who did, and with computer-aided design even his most complicated visions became feasible. A scrap of paper and a Perrier bottle could now become the basis for a building.

When it came to Bilbao, the design of the building, and the fabrication of the giant sheets of thin titanium which would glimmer like the scales of a fish lying on the city's waterfront, were a synthesis of art and technique, aesthetics and plumbing. When the museum opened to worldwide acclaim, it was recognized that Gehry's blend of energy and competence, his ability to bring a unique architectural vision to reality, had achieved its breakthrough. He was sixty-nine.

6. Closing the Experience Gap

If you were to map the link between productivity and age for almost every kind of work, it would follow an inverted U. Children have neither the energy nor competence to be lawyers. People over sixty are less likely to have the stamina and strength to work on construction sites. The peak for entrepreneurs is usually thought to be young middle age. But the shape and peak of the inverted U varies between activities. The young may have snappier short-term memories and greater facility with complex problems. But the reason why judges tend to be older is that they have acquired sound judgement through experience. 'Tacit knowledge' – the kind of knowledge that is hard to share, such as knowledge around trust and friendship evolved through experience – peaks in our fifties. As you think about being an entrepreneur, you have to think about the inverted U of productivity and age in the industry you are trying to enter, and where you lie on it.[15]

Another way to think about the ideals of age and experience for entrepreneurs is to consider the examples of Google and Facebook, both founded by young men in their early twenties who reached out early in their companies' existence for adult supervision.

Larry Page and Sergey Brin were still graduate students at Stanford University when they first tried raising money for their new search engine. Around midnight one night in the summer of 1998, they emailed Andy Bechtolsheim, an engineer who co-founded Sun Microsystems, asking to see him. Bechtolsheim wrote right back and told them to meet him at 8 a.m. the next morning at a friend's house on his way to work. He was impressed by what he saw, wrote a cheque for $100,000, and said he had to run.[16]

'We don't have a bank account yet,' Brin said.

'Deposit it when you get one,' said Bechtolsheim as he roared away in his Porsche. Page and Brin celebrated with breakfast at Burger King. Page then failed to deposit the cheque for a month.

The history of Google's early years is full of such stories. When that initial $100,000 started to run out, Page and Brin hired a young Stanford pre-med student, Salar Kamangar, to put together a pitch for investors. Brin was so dismissive of the whole process he had to ask Kamangar what a business plan was. At meetings with venture capitalists, the two founders frequently refused to answer questions they found intrusive. But the good investors were intrigued. John Doerr of Kleiner Perkins Caulfield & Byers, the pre-eminent Silicon Valley VC of the late 1990s, asked at the end of their first meeting what they thought their business might one day be worth. 'Ten billion,' said Page. Doerr was stunned. A market capitalization of a billion dollars would have been a huge hit. 'Oh, I'm very serious,' Page continued. 'And I don't mean market cap. I mean revenues.' 'I didn't think the guy could do it, but I was impressed,' Doerr said. 'It had to do with the tone of voice. He wasn't saying this to impress me or himself. This is what he believed. This was Larry's ambition, in a very thoughtful, considered way.'

The only problem would be building an organization to get to that goal. It wasn't just that the Google guys were slow to deposit a cheque.

They were fascinated by the engineering challenge they had set themselves, less by the business. If there was time to burn, they would spend it considering space travel instead of the business model.

Two years after Google had accepted $25 million in venture money, it was getting millions of search requests on its site each day, but had yet to make any money. Its main venture investors, Doerr and Mike Moritz of Sequoia, urged Page and Brin to hire a more seasoned CEO. When they bristled, Doerr decided to show them what they were missing, by organizing meetings with an all-star cast of technology leaders, including Jeff Bezos of Amazon, Steve Jobs of Apple and Andy Grove of Intel.

Doerr also knew that one of Page's haunting fears was suffering the fate of Nikola Tesla, whose career straddled the nineteenth and twentieth centuries. Tesla arrived in the United States from Serbia and worked briefly for Thomas Edison before striking out on his own. He was a pioneer in the use of electric power and wireless communication. He secured patents and even investment, but he could never build a proper business. As he grew older, he flitted from one New York hotel room to another, seized by paranoia that spies were trying to steal his work. He died poor and alone. Such was the fate of a scientist, however brilliant, who could not commercialize his inventions.

Page and Brin were convinced by the meetings Doerr arranged. But there was only one man they wanted: Jobs. When Doerr told them Jobs was committed to Apple, he urged them to meet Eric Schmidt, then forty-six and CEO of Novell, a networking company. Schmidt had the engineering chops to fit in at Google. He had earned a PhD in computer science at Berkeley and created his own coding tool. He

Nikola Tesla. A cautionary tale of innovation without entrepreneurship.

also had years of corporate experience, and to Page's delight, was also the only candidate to have attended the Burning Man festival in the Nevada desert. Schmidt was hired and remained as CEO for the next ten years while Google's revenues and profits exploded. He behaved more like a visiting professor than a hard-charging CEO, as he took care never to overshadow the founders who had hired him. It was not until 20 January 2011 that he stepped aside to become Executive Chairman and let Page became CEO. That day he tweeted: 'Day-to-day adult supervision no longer needed!'

A similar story unfolded at Facebook, which for the first few years of its existence reflected the personalities of its founder, Mark Zuckerberg, and his friends and fellow programmers: intense, engineering focussed and a little shabby round the edges. Zuckerberg was brimming with ideas about building a new kind of company, as big as any, but retaining the intimacy and fluid communication of a start-up. But he was awkward at meetings, and would break out into a sweat if he had to speak in public. As with Google, there were no concerns about the talent at Facebook, only about whether its executives had the nous to build an organization.

During the Christmas holidays of 2007, Zuckerberg met Sheryl Sandberg, who was as poised as he was edgy. She was fifteen years older, had worked at McKinsey, the World Bank and the US Treasury, obtained an MBA at Harvard and then helped to build Google's profit engine, AdWords. Within a few weeks of their first meeting, Sandberg agreed to join Facebook as its CEO. She brought a streak of elegance to an office full of young men in sweatshirts and hoodies, and an enviable contacts book ranging from Washington to New York to Los Angeles and back up through Silicon Valley. During the years following her arrival, Facebook began to hum, hiring more staff, adding more users and finally starting to churn out money, until in 2012 it launched the biggest Initial Public Offering in the history of technology.

What Zuckerberg did with Sheryl Sandberg and what Page and Brin did with Eric Schmidt was move themselves more quickly up that inverted U-curve of productivity and age. They hired the experience they needed, the tacit knowledge required to build a technology business. They brought forward their own crossing points of age and experience to create an explosion of maximum entrepreneurial energy and maximum competence which they could not have achieved alone.

II. A Brief History of an Idea

Entrepreneurship is a quicksilver term, less manageable and manipulable than the standard economic tools. Given a choice, most economists would rather worry at a high level about interest rates and levels of unemployment, bond prices and equity returns, than try to understand what occurs when individuals start and grow new businesses. They turn green amidst the disorder of entrepreneurship, the failure rates, the showmanship, the turbulence of it all. But in order to think like an entrepreneur, it is useful to know what the word actually means.

In 1730, Richard Cantillon, an Irish-French economist, introduced the concept of the entrepreneur as a force in economic life in his 'Essay on the Nature of Trade in General'. Two hundred years later, the Austrian economist Joseph Schumpeter reintroduced it forcefully in his book *Capitalism, Socialism and Democracy*, arguing that trying to write economic theory with no mention of entrepreneurs was 'like *Hamlet* without the Danish prince'.

The entrepreneur was originally thought to be a manager of risk, a businessperson who bought goods from a supplier with no guarantee that they could be sold. During the eighteenth century, to be in business was to be a merchant of some kind, or to be self-employed producing your own goods. But with the Industrial Revolution, business became more complex and so too did the definition and work of the entrepreneur. Entrepreneurs were no longer just risk-takers, but also innovators, people who instigated new ventures. They came to symbolize independence from the burgeoning industrial organizations. The entrepreneur was the person who broke free of the usual employer–employee relationships and struck out on his own.

In the United States, the entrepreneur took his philosophical lead from the rugged individualism which had been around since the early days of the colonies, when men and women from Europe had to chisel lives out of their new continent. This later merged with the writings of the Transcendentalists, men like Ralph Waldo Emerson and Henry David Thoreau, who believed that people were fundamentally good and became corrupted by the bogus rules and demands of society, by cities, businesses and money.

In an essay titled 'Self-Reliance', Emerson wrote:

The civilized man has built a coach, but has lost the use of his feet. He is supported on crutches, but lacks so much support of muscle. He has a fine Geneva watch, but he fails of the skill to tell the hour by the sun. A Greenwich nautical almanac he has, and so being sure of the information when he wants it, the man in the street does not know a star in the sky. The solstice he does not observe; the equinox he knows as little; and the whole bright calendar of the year is without a dial in his mind. His note-books impair his memory; his libraries overload his wit; the insurance-office increases the number of accidents; and it may be a question whether machinery does not encumber; whether we have not lost by refinement some energy, by a Christianity entrenched in establishments and forms, some vigor of wild virtue.

He railed against conformity and 'foolish consistency', the 'hobgoblin of little minds', and urged people to look inwards for inspiration, 'to detect and watch that gleam of light which flashes across his mind from within'. 'It is easy in the world to live after the world's opinion,' he wrote. 'It is easy in solitude to live after our own; but the great man is he who in the midst of a crowd keeps with perfect sweetness the independence of solitude.' Steve Jobs was so taken by this essay and its theme of self-reliance that he named his personal foundation the Emerson Collective.

Henry David Thoreau famously retreated to a shack beside Walden Pond in Massachusetts to escape the debauched comforts of city life and 'to live deliberately, to front only the essential facts of life, and see if I could not learn what it had to teach, and not, when I came to die, discover that I had not lived'. Thoreau's writing veers between an exciting individualism and shrill solipsism. He railed against the tyranny of busy work, but ranted as vehemently against small talk as a form of escape from oneself. Those things which engage most men, he wrote, such as politics, business, travel and conversation, should be 'unconsciously performed, like the corresponding functions of the physical body' as they are 'infra-human, a kind of vegetation'.

By the late nineteenth century, large-scale industry and huge organizations were thriving. Once the United States was bound together by railroads, these organizations blossomed to serve this vast, single market. Salesmen could now crisscross the entire country selling the same suits, steaks and soap powder. The fortunes of the

From Emerson and Thoreau to Steve Jobs, stepping away from the throng creates a steely self-reliance.

American Gilded Age were the result of the emergence of opportunities which could be attacked at vast scale: steel making, railway building, canal building, coal mining, industrial agriculture, and all the financial wizardry required to fund them.

In this new environment, the entrepreneur was more than just a manager of risk, or a thrifty small businessman making his solitary way in a still rough-and-tumble society. He now had the opportunity to become a titan, a figure like John D. Rockefeller, the founder of Standard Oil and the richest man in history. Rockefeller had some of the traits of America's early, Puritan colonists. He never drank alcohol or smoked, and was a devout Baptist. But he was also a sharp-elbowed capitalist who believed that business was a matter of 'survival of the fittest'.

It took an Austrian, Schumpeter, to recognize the entrepreneur's new role in the American economy, and he did so in the 1930s, amidst the ruins of the Great Depression. Schumpeter had grown up in the Vienna of the Austro-Hungarian Empire. In 1919, in the wake of the First World War, he was briefly Austria's Finance Minister. He then spent five years as a banker in the private sector, an experience which turned sour and left him badly in debt. He took up an itinerant career as an academic economist, teaching in Europe, Japan and America before settling at Harvard in 1932. He believed that to understand economics, you needed to know more history than mathematics. You needed to understand culture and psychology as much as the stimulative effect of government borrowing.

It must have been quite an experience to attend one of Joseph Schumpeter's economics classes at Harvard in those years. A fastidious figure, with a gleaming bald head and elegantly cut suits, he would stride into classes of timid undergraduates and announce: 'As a young man, I set myself three goals. To be the greatest economist in the world, the best horseman in Austria and the greatest lover in Vienna.' Then as the class settled down, he would murmur that had it not been for the stern competition among Austria's horsemen, he would have achieved all three. It was a boast to set his students off-kilter and a goad that they should pursue only their loftiest ambitions.

Schumpeter argued that growth in an economy was instigated by entrepreneurs whose role was 'to reform or revolutionize the pattern of production by exploiting an invention or, more generally, an untried technological possibility for producing a new commodity or producing an old one in a new way, by opening up a new source of supply of materials or a new outlet for products, by reorganizing an industry and so on'.[1] He said that the dynamic process of change and wealth creation required the destruction of whatever existed before, and thus blew a 'perennial gale of creative destruction', a phrase which has both inspired entrepreneurs and terrified entrenched businesses and policymakers ever since. Where you stand on Schumpeter often depends on whether you are in the creation business or vulnerable to destruction.

It is worth pausing for a moment to consider Schumpeter's description of entrepreneurship as reforming or revolutionizing the pattern of production. He does not equate the entrepreneur with the inventor. To make a scientific discovery or technological breakthrough is one thing. To commercialize it is the work of the entrepreneur. Henry Ford did not invent the automobile, but he created the organization to make cars at sufficient scale so that millions of Americans could afford one. Richard Branson did not invent the transatlantic passenger flight when he launched Virgin Atlantic in 1984. But he did reorganize the industry.

Virgin Atlantic released a wonderful television commercial in 2009 to mark its twenty-fifth anniversary.[2] It opens in 1984 with a newspaper vendor calling out news of the miners' strike and a young businessman pulling up to Heathrow airport, talking into a brick-sized mobile phone. Then in the grey of the terminal, he spies a flash of blonde hair, then a polished red heel and then through the dull throng a line of Virgin hostesses in their scarlet uniforms, striding arm in arm like supermodels, all brilliant teeth, bouncing manes and long, long legs. A couple of frumpy, rival air hostesses shake their heads, a nerd turns, awestruck, from his space-invaders game, a man squirts ketchup down his shirt front. One passenger turns to another and says: 'I need to change my job.' The other man says: 'I need to change my ticket.' It is that word 'change', repeated and evident in every aspect of the commercial, which tells us that this was a moment of entrepreneurial innovation.

Schumpeter's theory of entrepreneurship, however, then took a grim twist. He believed that the pressures of creative destruction led to the creation of monopolies, as only monopoly returns were sufficient to inspire risk-taking entrepreneurship. And once these monopolies were in place, they became bureaucratic and more adept at self-preservation than innovation. The corporatists froze out the individualists, and an economy went from thrusting and modern to traditional and self-preserving. He wrote that the 'critical frame of mind . . . after having destroyed the moral authority of so many institutions, in the end turns against its own' and the corporation 'although the product of the capitalist process, socializes the bourgeois mind; it relentlessly narrows the scope of capitalist motivation . . . [and] will eventually kill its roots.'

By the 1970s, it seemed like his prediction had come true. Many economists believed that entrepreneurs had become trivial to economic life, overwhelmed by the might of corporations. Only big companies had the muscle to innovate on a scale that mattered. No puny individual could mount a challenge to giants like IBM in computers or Eastman Kodak in photography, with their near-monopoly positions, managerial know-how and lavishly funded research divisions.

What these economists underestimated was popular resistance to any form of status quo. While it is true that entrepreneurial firms once successful can become tyrannical monopolies, it is equally true that in dynamic markets those firms quickly become targets for the next crop of pesky entrepreneurs. The sclerosis the economists feared did not prove inevitable. The idea of the entrepreneur, though weakened, still had a pulse. But it required another Austrian-born economist, Peter Drucker, to get it back on its feet.

Drucker was twenty-six years younger than Schumpeter, but his career followed a similar arc. He was educated in Vienna but left between the World Wars and settled in the United States, becoming a professor at New York University and later Claremont University, just outside Los Angeles. He was a truculent and independent thinker, who, like Schumpeter, saw economics as a bruising field of human endeavour, populated by thinking, feeling people rather than ruled by scientific formulae. He reckoned that entrepreneurship was a learn-able behaviour, a systematic process of 'purposeful innovation'. This process can be followed by an ambitious individual, a large corporation, a charity or even a government department. He thus liberated our understanding of entrepreneurship from the narrow confines of business and capitalism.

Innovation, he wrote, was the 'specific instrument of entrepreneurship . . . the act that endows resources with a new capacity to create wealth'. Fossil fuels were lying under man's feet for millennia before we figured out how to extract them and use them to power machines. Innovations in mining, extraction and processing led by entrepreneurs turned these mineral resources into sources of wealth and human progress. The personal computer existed before Bill Gates, but he figured out what software they required to run on every office desk in the world, and a business model to match.

The first example of systematic entrepreneurship, according to Drucker, was the Crédit Mobilier bank founded by the Péreire brothers in France in 1857. Its purpose was to mobilize other people's money to invest in areas of higher productivity. Unlike the Rothschilds of that time, the Péreires did not seek to own what they invested in. They made their money by pulling in money from the public, investing it in early-stage opportunities in mining, railways and new forms of financial institution and then cashing in once the business had proved a success to look for another opportunity. It was an early form of venture capital intended to fund companies which would change the economy.

But Drucker also identified entrepreneurial behaviour in other fields. He wrote of the development of American universities, which began with European models but quickly morphed into many different forms to serve different markets, age groups and demographics. He also noted entrepreneurship in the evolution of hospitals, from community hospitals to specialized treatment centres to the emergence of vast healthcare organizations.

Entrepreneurs according to Drucker's definition need not be capitalists or investors. They can be employers or employees. The risks they take and the uncertainty they face are not materially different from those experienced by people with responsibility in almost any profession, whether in politics, the military, or captaining a cruise ship. All kinds of people, he observed, could meet entrepreneurial challenges. What marked them out was not a personality or behavioural trait, but a way of seeking out and making decisions. 'The entrepreneur,' he wrote, 'always searches for change, responds to it, and exploits it as an opportunity.'[3]

It is the three steps of searching, responding and exploiting an opportunity laid out by Drucker, and which define the entrepreneur, that we shall explore next.

III. Searching for Opportunity

1. The Adjacent Possible

In 1958, a young white man found himself lost and stranded in a Jamaican mangrove forest. He walked for miles in blazing heat, until he found a hut in a clearing. An old Rastafarian man, with long, twisted dreadlocks, poked his head out. The young man was terrified. Rastafarians were considered dangerous, rebellious figures in Jamaica. But he was so thirsty, he asked for a drink of water. The old man handed him a gourd and the young man drank and fell fast asleep. A few hours later, he woke to see a group of Rastafarians surrounding him. He was terrified again, but one of the men offered to take him home and his fear of this ostracized group of Jamaicans turned to fascination.

Chris Blackwell was nineteen when this happened. He was working at a hotel in Jamaica owned by his cousins and managing a water-skiing concession. The following year, he used an inheritance to begin travelling back and forth to London and New York, bringing back jazz and blues records to Jamaica, and selling ska to Jamaican immigrants overseas. In 1963, he began looking for a crossover record, one he could sell in all of his markets, and found a fifteen-year-old Jamaican singer, Millie Small. Their song 'My Boy Lollipop' sold 7 million copies.

Over the next decade, Blackwell built up his own record company with acts like Steve Winwood and Roxy Music, and bands playing reggae, the music of his native Jamaica. In 1971, a local band from

Kingston came to see Blackwell in frustration at their existing recording deal. Blackwell knew Bob Marley and the Wailers and gave them an advance on their next album, *Catch a Fire*. For the next eight years, Marley and his band recorded a series of ever-more-popular albums. The image, music and language of Jamaica's Rastafarians became beloved around the world.

Chris Blackwell later discovered U2 as well, and sold his record company, Island, in 1989 for $300 million. He made a second fortune buying up and developing property in Miami's South Beach and continues to develop hotels in the Caribbean. But the origin of that interest in Rastafarians was something no professor of business could have predicted.

The search for an entrepreneurial opportunity is often couched in terms of creativity and inspiration. But the data points to a much more humdrum reality. Nearly three-quarters of entrepreneurs find their ideas while in their current job. A fifth find them by chance and fewer than 5 per cent by systematically searching for new opportunities.[1]

It makes perfect sense that most entrepreneurs discover opportunities in the work that surrounds them, in 'the adjacent possible', a phrase coined by the theoretical biologist Stuart Kauffman.[2] They succeed by doing something they know about. If they are pipe-fitters, they figure out an improvement to the way pipe-fitting is done. If they are coders, they develop a business based on computer programming.

King Gillette came upon his idea to sell disposable razor blades from his experience selling bottle caps. If one could throw away a bottle cap and reuse a glass bottle, why not the same with razors? It struck him one morning in 1895.

One of history's great 'aha' moments.

As I stood there with the razor in my hand, my eyes resting on it as lightly as a bird settling down on its nest, the Gillette razor was born – more with the rapidity of a dream than by a process of reasoning. In a moment, I saw it all: the way the blade could be held in a holder; the idea of sharpening the two opposite edges on the thin piece of steel; the clamping plates for the blade, with a handle halfway between the two edges of the blade . . . I stood there before the mirror in a trance of joy. My wife was visiting Ohio and I hurriedly wrote to her: 'I've got it! Our fortune is made!'

Gillette still had to build a company, but he did so to great effect, creating a near monopoly which endured for years.

2. The Gossip Test

As World War II came to a close, a young scientist named Francis Crick wondered what he should do next. He was about to turn thirty and yet to settle on a career. He had obtained a second-class degree from University College London, and then spent a desultory couple of years researching what he considered 'the dullest problem imaginable', the viscosity of water under pressure. During the war, he had worked at the Admiralty designing mines for enemy shipping lanes. By the end, he wrote,

> I was reasonably sure that I didn't want to spend the rest of my life designing weapons, but what did I want to do? I took stock of my qualifications. A not-very-good degree redeemed somewhat by my achievements at the Admiralty. A knowledge of certain restricted parts of magnetism and hydrodynamics, neither of them subjects for which I felt the least bit of enthusiasm. No published papers at all. The few short Admiralty reports I had written . . . would count for very little. Only gradually did I realize that this lack of qualification could be an advantage. By the time most scientists have reached age thirty they are trapped by their own expertise. They have invested so much effort in one particular field that it is often extremely difficult at that time in their careers to make a

radical change. I, on the other hand, knew nothing, except for a basic training in somewhat old-fashioned physics and mathematics and an ability to turn my hand to new things.[3]

Crick went to see Georg Kreisel, a friend and eminent mathematical logician. When Crick proposed a career in fundamental scientific research, Kreisel weighed the matter logically and advised, 'I've known a lot of people more stupid than you who've made a success of it.' But what to study? Crick felt that he was too old to make a mistake. If he wasted three years studying a subject which went nowhere, he would run out of time to change course again. The scientific career ladder is inaccessible after a certain age. As he wandered the halls of the Admiralty, chatting to colleagues, he observed that he ended up talking a great about the thriving field of antibiotics. He knew very little about it, besides what he had read casually in periodicals, but realized he was not just talking about science the way he talked about mines and water density. He was gossiping about it.

'I had discovered the gossip test – what you are really interested in is what you gossip about. Without hesitation, I applied it to my recent conversations.' Now he narrowed down his interests to the brain and the 'borderline between the living and the nonliving'. What these areas had in common, he realized, was that they touched on subjects often thought beyond the realm of science, areas often left to religion. He chose molecular biology because he felt that his faith in science and disbelief in religious dogma would fuel the dedication he required to succeed. This was the first step on the path which would lead him to the Nobel Prize for his co-discovery, with James Watson, of the double-helical structure of DNA.

3. A Bug Named Jim

The management writer Jim Collins was a studious child, who kept a notebook and filled it with observations about the world around him. He would catch an insect, put it in a jar, and watch it for days, noting what it ate, how it walked, how long it slept. As an adult, he took a job at Hewlett Packard, a good job at a prestigious firm. Yet for reasons he could not isolate, he felt dissatisfied. Rather than simply languishing like most of us, Collins bought a fresh notebook, the kind he had used as a boy, and began to observe himself as if he were a bug in a jar. He described his working day and the moments he enjoyed and those he disliked. Over the course of a year, he discovered that he was happiest when he was teaching and analysing complex systems, so he decided to quit his job and pursue a career in academia. He joined the faculty at the Stanford Business School and eventually wrote a series of bestselling management books about the secrets of successful companies.

This process of intense self-observation and self-awareness is vital to anyone thinking of embarking on an entrepreneurial adventure.

4. Shifts and Disruptions

A cartoon published in the *New Yorker* in 1974 shows a woman gushing to a smug-looking man: 'Dynamite, Mr Gerston! You're the first person I ever heard use "paradigm" in real life.' Over the previous decade, the word 'paradigm' had lurched from the byways of scientific history into the managerial mainstream, courtesy of Thomas Kuhn, a physicist-turned-historian at the University of California at Berkeley. Professor Kuhn was a doctoral student at Harvard in 1947 when he was asked to teach a science course to undergraduates studying humanities. In preparation, he read Aristotle's *Physics*. How, he wondered, could such a brilliant man have been so wrong about so much? He pondered this question for the next fifteen years and eventually wrote that the reason was not that Aristotle was wrong and Newton right. It was that they thought within entirely different paradigms. These paradigms were models of thought, which made sound internal sense, until one day they didn't. All the scientists who trusted that the sun revolved around the earth worked on theories which made sense within that paradigm, until Copernicus showed otherwise.

Once James Watson and Francis Crick discovered the molecular structure of DNA, the paradigm of molecular biology shifted to allow a new era of genetic experimentation. Crick made an ideal paradigm-shifter, because as he observed about himself, he came to academic science relatively late, without the expectations and intellectual shackles of those who had been immersed in it since their early twenties. He was not indoctrinated. He was sufficiently independent of the existing paradigm to smash it.

But how, as an entrepreneur, are you to figure out whether the paradigm you are operating within is a good one which will serve you well, or one you would be better served destroying?

The Super Bowl trophy awarded each year to the champions of America's National Football League is named after Vince Lombardi, who coached the Green Bay Packers to victory in the first two Super Bowls, played in 1966 and 1967. Lombardi believed in military discipline, pride and perfect execution of even the tiniest details of his sport. To emphasize the simplicity of his methods and the clarity of his goals, he would gather his players on the first day of preseason training each year and hold up a football. 'Gentlemen,' he would announce, '*this* is a football.'

The paradigm for Packers football was simple. Discipline, strength and hard work led to results. You wore down the opposition with brute strength and will.

But what if you didn't have that kind of team? What if your quarterback couldn't sling the ball way downfield and the giant brutes you wanted kept being recruited by other teams? What if you were constrained by your budget and the talents at your disposal from competing under that paradigm? This was the challenge for Bill Walsh, a wilful, nervy character who took over the San Francisco 49ers in 1979.

The 49ers was a struggling team, with ramshackle facilities and a lowly regarded roster of players. Walsh could have stuck to the prevailing NFL paradigm and failed. Instead he began to chip away at it. He had a young quarterback in Joe Montana who was nimble and intelligent but not gifted with a rocket of an arm. So Walsh turned the game in his favour. He turned it from 'checkers to chess'. He learned to conceal his plays from the opposition by switching players to different positions right up to the moment when play began. Whereas most teams concentrated their force on the centre of the field, Walsh ordered passes sent out to the edges, where there was more room to run. He turned the orderly ground-war of football into an aerial bombardment, full of short, zippy passes, feints and darting runs.

'For my effort in coming up with a successful new way of doing things, I received the disparagement of many in the NFL,' he wrote, 'especially old-timers who dismissively called it the nickel-and-dime, dink-and-dunk, fancy-pants, or finesse offense – even the swish-and-sway. Their condescension stemmed from the fact that my approach didn't rely on the traditional brute-force, grinding-ground game, or spectacular "long-bomb" pass of old-time NFL football. It wasn't physical enough for them . . . In a sense the naysayers were seeking victory, but only if it came the old-fashioned way. They were locked into the past and unwittingly locking themselves out of the future. Leaders do this to themselves and their organizations all the time.'[4]

But for all the criticism at the time, Walsh's entrepreneurial efforts, forced on him by his team's limitations, yielded three Super Bowls during his ten years as head coach of the 49ers and he is reckoned now to have been one of the greatest coaches ever.

The term 'disruption' is used these days as often as 'paradigm shift' was in the 1970s. It's rare to meet an entrepreneur who isn't promising to disrupt one industry or another. I recently met a couple of teenagers working at an entrepreneurial accelerator whose goal was to 'disrupt retail' by launching a new kind of coffee shop/hangout where you could buy everything from the mugs to the sofas and the art on the walls. But that is not disruption. That is simply a new kind of coffee shop.

Disruption is a specific process which every entrepreneur needs to understand, because not every start-up needs to be disruptive to be a wild success. But if you do plan to disrupt an existing industry, it is useful to know the theory before you launch into practice.[5]

Disruption occurs in three phases, which can take many years to play out. Imagine first a large corporation, decades old and entrenched in its ways. It has a glossy headquarters and executives who fly around the world in private jets. It has thousands of employees and its advertising underwrites global events like the Olympics. All of these trappings cost money, and they are paid for by products which for years have generated colossal profits. But over time, this corporation has added layers. First, they made perfect sense: an accounting department to deal with all the money flowing in and out; research and development to create new products and improve the existing ones; legal to deal with regulatory issues; and marketing to keep up with the slew of new opportunities to present the company's products. But slowly, these layers became self-justifying and self-reinforcing. The link between the value created by the company's products and the economic value created by each employee erodes. And the consequences of this erosion start to work their way back into the products, which become more complicated than consumers need simply to justify the now-sprawling organization. Suddenly, a crack opens in the market, usually amongst the least regarded or even ignored consumers, and it is here the disruptor first enters.

In 1965, the computer market was dominated by mainframes sold by IBM. These were expensive hunks of technology which filled entire rooms and required costly servicing and upgrades. IBM's salesforce, in their uniform of dark blue suits and ties and crisp white shirts, were there to take your cheque and hold your hand. But for small and midsized businesses which could not afford an IBM mainframe, an alternative began to emerge: minicomputers. Much cheaper and smaller, they ran on different software and performed a simpler set of tasks. Over the next two decades, these minicomputers improved and became personal computers. Their software improved too, and because of their cost and open architectures, they attracted a more fluid and creative group of innovators. The mainframe companies kept improving their own offerings, trying to defend their profits. But gradually more and more businesses looked at the improving mini and personal computers and wondered why they were paying so much for their expensive mainframes when they could get more of what they needed for less. But still, it took until the early 1990s for the minicomputer market to pass the mainframe market once and for all and force it into decline.

One of the hardest lessons for companies which get disrupted is that they could see the threat coming, and simply mishandled it. No one knew more about the possibilities of digital photography than Kodak, yet in order to preserve its lucrative print business, Kodak hung on to its old model and eventually went bankrupt. Newspapers were alive to the possibilities and threats of digital publishing, but spent much of the 1990s and well into the 2000s trying to protect their existing profits. They built their own websites and offered online advertising deals to their usual customers, car companies and department stores. But they were missing what Internet advertising was all about: individualization. Companies like Google could now tell you who was looking at your advertising and how they responded, and bill you accordingly. And they didn't have the cost of sustaining newspaper bureaus all over the world.

The classified-advertising industry was similarly upended, as you no longer needed to pay for an ad in a newspaper and wait for it to come out. You could now write your ad, add a photograph, and post it on Craigslist for free, and know that anyone with an Internet connection could see it.

The editors at newspapers were committed to a particular kind of product, and their ad-sales teams were committed to particular kinds of relationships with their customers, while the Internet was creating an entirely different media universe of buyers and sellers, engaged in low-cost direct marketing, right alongside them.

Again, we see the three phases of disruption: direct marketing becomes available to a new group of customers for whom it had previously been too expensive or complicated; the new group grows to include customers of the established business wondering why they are still paying for what they no longer need; the established business goes into decline.

Entrepreneurial thinking about disruption requires not just thinking about the right product – an inexpensive razor to replace the costly four-bladed blade of the moment – but also about attacking the prevailing modes of doing business. Businesses can become attached to behaviours which have nothing to do with the consumer. If you are a publisher who has spent thirty years enjoying long lunches and days at the races with the executives who bought advertising in your newspaper, it is difficult to accept that companies can now get straight to consumers through a search engine. They don't need your platform any more, and they certainly don't need your prices and your champagne. There is nothing more terrifying to the well-padded corporate executive than the thought of having to give up all those hard-acquired perks simply in order to survive. That period of denial is the moment for the disruptive entrepreneur to attack.

One final example of disruption from an unexpected field. Until the 1960s, if the arteries around your heart clogged up, your prognosis was poor. Then came coronary-bypass surgery, a complex, expensive but often successful procedure which allowed surgeons to crack open a patient's ribs, stop their heart and reroute blood flow around a constricted artery. It was painful and recovery could take months, but it could prolong lives by years. Then in 1974, a young German doctor, Andreas Gruentzig, performed the first balloon angioplasty. This involved sending a catheter into a blocked coronary artery, inflating a small balloon to push the artery open, then removing the catheter. It was a much simpler, less gory procedure, and could be performed by cardiologists as well as cardiac surgeons. At first cardiac surgeons dismissed it. It was not useful to people with seriously blocked arteries. And if it was so simple a cardiologist could do it, it did not seem worthy of their time. It was also reimbursed by insurance companies at a much lower rate than full-blown open-heart surgery.

For years, balloon angioplasty was used on a new market of patients, those with mild blockages in their coronary arteries. Until the 1990s, the frequency of both bypass surgery and angioplasty grew as treatments for heart disease multiplied and improved. Phase 1 of disruption. But eventually, angioplasty's advantages, its lower cost, its relative simplicity, and the reduced trauma for patients, moved it ahead of surgery. It became even more effective with the arrival of stents, metal cages which could be slipped into an artery to hold it open for longer. This meant it could be used on patients who previously had to be treated with bypass surgery. Phase 2. In Phase 3, cardiologists have vastly expanded the market of patients, taking on much of the work which used to be done by cardiac surgeons, who now operate only on the most critical cases.[6]

Disruption can occur in all kinds of fields and can be exploited by the canny entrepreneur. But it does not just mean change, or unleashing the forces of chaos upon order. It refers to this specific three-phase process. Those with everything to lose respond to the waves of disruption by trying to bail out their fatally holed craft. The entrepreneur pulls out a surfboard.

5. The Slow Hunch

Inventions, even when they seem like flashes of inspiration, emerge from the vast mass of human experience. As knowledge accrues, so do the possibilities of discovering the new. Each generation stands atop a larger body of information and experience. Even the paradigm-shifters who stand a little to one side of the formal way of doing things at least have that formal approach from which to stage their shift. You cannot shift a paradigm which isn't there in the first place.

This glacial process of invention leading to invention leads us to another way of thinking about the pursuit of opportunity, as a 'slow hunch' which evolves in the mind of an entrepreneur over time. The author Steven Johnson has popularized this idea and calls the slow hunch the 'anti-lightbulb moment', as it describes an idea which comes into focus over many years.[7] He describes the work of Clarence Birdseye, the father of frozen food. In 1912, when Birdseye was twenty-five, he moved his family to Labrador, in the Canadian province of Newfoundland, where he sold furs and pursued his work as a naturalist. In order to feed his young son during the frigid winter, he learned from the local Inuit how to ice-fish, dropping a line through a hole in a frozen lake. He observed that when he pulled out a trout, it froze within seconds of contact with the air. When he thawed it out later, he observed, the fish still tasted fresh. He staged a series of experiments to discover why and found that the secret lay in the speed of the freezing. If you froze food very quickly, you did less damage to it than if you froze it slowly, so it tasted fresher when you eventually thawed it.

When he returned from Labrador to New York, Birdseye joined the Fisheries Association, and was disgusted by the filth and waste of commercial fishing, and decided that freezing might offer an answer. Frozen food was considered unfit even for prison inmates at the time, as freezing technology was so shoddy. It took Birdseye another decade to figure out how to freeze food consistently and at scale so it retained the freshness he found in his Labrador trout. But by the mid 1920s he had cracked it. Shortly before the Wall Street crash of 1929, he sold his thriving frozen-food company, General Seafood, for millions. As Johnson points out, all kinds of influences went into Birdseye's success. His curiosity for nature and willingness to move his wife and newborn son to frozen Labrador; his experience of commercial fisheries; his determination to build a production line inspired by Henry Ford's factories for the Model T car.

'Like every idea,' Johnson writes, 'Birdseye's breakthrough was not a single insight, but a network of other ideas, packaged together in a new configuration. What made Birdseye's idea so powerful was not simply his individual genius, but the diversity of places and forms of expertise that he brought together.'

IV. Responding to Opportunity

1. Assembling Complementary Assets

The economist Ronald Coase said that a company forms a natural boundary at the point at which it becomes less expensive for it to perform an activity itself than to pay someone outside. If it is cheaper to own its own warehouses, it adds a warehousing division. If not, it rents from someone else. If it is less expensive to have an accountant in-house, it hires an accountant rather than using an outside firm. An entrepreneur considering how to pursue an opportunity must think the same way about what economists call 'complementary assets'. How do you pursue the opportunity in the way you want to? Is it by working inside an organization which has abundant, existing resources? Or by establishing your own, and going out and raising money and hiring people? You can be entrepreneurial either way.

Let's start with a very simple kind of entrepreneurial endeavour: a food truck. You will need some basic cooking skills, the money to buy a truck, a permit, a place to park and some way of marketing yourself. The complementary assets are fairly simple to acquire, and you don't need to be part of a giant chain of food trucks, or to employ dozens of staff to turn your idea into reality.

But then consider a much more complex opportunity. Say you are a university research scientist who has discovered a drug which can prolong the lives of pancreatic-cancer sufferers by six months. You have several options. You can patent your drug and then set up a company to take it through the many years and rounds of government-required testing before it can come to market. You will have to raise the money for those tests and for the staff you will now have to hire to keep your research moving forward. And this is assuming your university does not try to claim that the intellectual property on the drug is theirs, as you discovered it in their labs, at their expense. Or, you can submit your resignation to your university and join a large pharmaceutical company, which promises to pay you a large salary and give you a piece of any future profits from the drug. They have the staff and money to support a long regulatory-approval process, and the sales and marketing teams to deliver your treatment to those who most need it.

By joining the pharmaceutical company, you may be foregoing your chance to become a billionaire and build the next great drug company. But you may be increasing the chance of your drug coming to market, and sparing yourself all the hassle of building an organization when your time might be better spent in the laboratory.

Writers are faced with a similar conundrum in these days of self-publishing. In theory, all that separates a writer from an audience is a keystroke. So publishers have to make a case for the value of their complementary assets: their editors, publicists, book designers, access to reviewers, blurbs, and their dominance over the main sales and marketing channels online and off. They can craft a book's words, package it beautifully and make sure it sits on the front table of the chain bookstores. You can certainly go it alone as a writer these days, but why not focus on the writing and let the publishers do the work? The writer must weigh the potential of going it alone versus the advantages of collaborating with an established publisher.

If enthusiasm and self-awareness have brought you this far as an entrepreneur, the moment when you first respond to the opportunity you have discovered is the moment at which you become a managerial decision-maker.

2. People

Corporate executives spend their days trying to manage volume. Their inboxes are swollen, their calendars full. The successful ones find ways to eliminate the chaff and focus on what is important. If they waste their decision-making energy on endless small things, they won't have any left for the big decisions. Their skill is in deciding which of several options to pursue.

Entrepreneurs, by contrast, start out in silence. They are nobody with nothing to sell. There is no one forcing a hundred decisions on them. They have to conjure up their own decisions to make. This is often the reason people with corporate backgrounds struggle when they join a start-up. They no longer have several options to choose from each morning. They have to come up with the options in the first place. It is not just shall we price our product at this point or another, but do we have a product at all? Very quickly, however, that changes, and entrepreneurs are overwhelmed with decisions. They must make decisions which are right for the next twenty-four hours but which also take them along the path towards a five-year goal. Many of these decisions might seem small at the time, but could have long-term consequences. The most significant in this early stage involve people.

Three issues about people stand out here and they are worth lingering over.

The first involves working with friends and family. We all apply very different logic to the various relationships in our lives. We have friends and family and we have people we do business with. We apply a social logic to the former and a business logic to the latter. When you are starting a company, it is easy to get these two forms of logic tangled up. You hire friends and family because they are the people you trust, and they are the ones most supportive of your idea. Loneliness can kill a start-up and the enthusiasm and presence of friends is reassuring in those early, uncertain days. But unless there is a sound business logic for their presence, you could be in for trouble. These people are likely to think like you and will reinforce your prejudices rather than broaden your vision. They may not challenge you when challenge is just what you need. And they may be difficult to fire if they turn out to be poor employees. If you have accepted their money as a seed investment, you will have to answer to them over the dinner table if everything goes wrong.

A second issue is that of agents and stewards. Some people work for a salary and nothing more. They are agents of the company. Their loyalty will be limited, their commitment will extend no further than their precise job description, and they will expect to be paid a full market wage. Stewards are those who feel a sense of ownership. They feel their work has greater purpose beyond their immediate financial return. They are in it for the long haul, and will give you their nights and weekends if they have to. They will bleed for you and behave as if they own the company rather than simply work for it.

It is easy to imagine that equity holders think as stewards and employees as agents, but it is rarely so simple. You will have some investors who want to see the company grow quickly and be sold so they can realize a short, sharp financial return. Others will be willing to wait and see if your small start-up really can change the world as well as deliver billions of pounds in gains. You will issue equity to employees you covet in order to lure them away from a rival only to find they quit the moment they get a better offer. Meanwhile the humblest salary-earner will turn out to be putting in extra hours to ensure the product gets launched on time.

The third area of human relations which an entrepreneur must consider is their own willingness to deal with others and themselves with extreme, sometimes brutal honesty. Entrepreneurs have little time to waste and must constantly think in terms of their 'runway'. In their pre-revenue days, they can figure out the lifespan of their business by dividing their money on hand by their monthly expenses. If you've got £120,000 left and you are spending £10,000 a month, then you have twelve months of runway. Every decision you make can either lengthen or shorten that runway. If an employee isn't working out and you can save £3,000 a month by firing him today, you can extend your runway by nearly five months. Dither and you'll be another month closer to extinction, shoved off the entrepreneurial bandwagon and back to working for someone else.

Most of us know when a decision has to be made, but we put off making it because of the pain involved. The time lost in not making a necessary decision can be the time separating success from failure. The founders of Ocado, the British online grocer, raised £50 million in 2000 for their idea and quickly plunged £12 million into a monorail system to pick and pack orders speedily for customers. But when they realized the system would not work, they had to make a decision. Having spent the first decade of their careers on the trading floor at Goldman Sachs, they knew that when the facts change, you are better off taking your loss early. It will only become more expensive with time. To the astonishment of their investors, they decided to ditch the monorail and move on.[1]

Steve Jobs was notorious for his merciless criticism of employees. After one particularly brutal salvo against his colleagues, Jony Ive, Apple's head of design, protested. Jobs said, 'Why would you be vague?' Ambiguity, he said, was a form of selfishness: 'You don't care about how they *feel*! You're being vain, you want them to like you.' Ive was furious, but came to agree. 'It's really demeaning to think that, in this deep desire to be liked, you've compromised giving clear, unambiguous feedback,' he said. He lamented that there were 'so many anecdotes' about Jobs's acerbity because 'his intention, and motivation, wasn't to be hurtful'.[2] Not all of us are in such command of our own vanity.

People who work in large organizations are constantly making decisions of no importance whatsoever. Their opinions are diluted by others, their choices cut short by financial demands issued from on high, or delayed thanks to the luxury of fat profits and time. Most corporate decisions are disembodied, the product of cultures and crowds rather than individuals. Entrepreneurs get to see their decisions bear fruit. What they say goes, and that freedom, that actualization through action, is the thrill of what they do. Bruised feelings may be the price for retaining such a privilege.

3. Context

Since entrepreneurship is so often a matter of barrelling into the unknown, it helps to have a relationship to your landscape. It helps if people know you and trust you. If you are more than just a credit score to them. If they know your character. If you've done this before.

Entrepreneurs are unlike artists in that their work can be measured by objective criteria. A drill either bores a clean hole or it doesn't. A bank either conducts your financial affairs efficiently or it doesn't. You don't need taste to judge whether their products are a success. But there are some entrepreneurs who come closer to artists than others, because their success cannot solely be measured by their impact on the market. Chefs are a typical case, and context and trust are especially important for those wanting to achieve something unique.

At the age of forty-nine, Rose Gray was an improbable candidate to become one of England's most celebrated chefs. A few years earlier, she and her husband had left London for Italy after their business importing cast-iron stoves from Europe went bankrupt. In Tuscany, she had fallen in love with Italian food and the ways of finding ingredients locally and seasonally. But she had cooked professionally for only two years, at a nightclub restaurant in New York – unless you counted a brief phase making crêpes at parties in London when she was in her twenties.

Restaurants are a notoriously hard business, so it took a leap of faith from someone who knew her well to entrust her with a kitchen.

Some twenty years earlier, a young graphic artist from upstate New York had shown up in London looking for work and a place to live. Ruthie Elias ended up living with Gray and her family in Maida Vale, and soon married their friend, the architect Richard Rogers. In 1987, Ruthie was looking for a partner to open an Italian restaurant next to her husband's offices at Thames Wharf in Hammersmith. It would help turn the still-evolving development into more of a community. Richard, who is Italian by birth, and his architects could come and eat food prepared by his wife. Ruthie proposed the idea to Rose over a cup of coffee and Rose accepted with a 'let's do it'.[3]

It was just the two of them at first, plus a waiter and someone to wash the dishes. But after five years they were able to expand and grow a herb and vegetable garden outside the dining room. By 1998, they had their first Michelin star, had published a best-selling recipe book and were presenting a television series, *The Italian Kitchen*. The staff were an unusual crew, as Gray and Rogers never insisted on their chefs being formally trained. They were allowed to come in and show what they could do, to reveal their talents as well as their temperament. 'Cook me a dessert,' Rose would say to a newcomer at the end of a lunch service. If it was good enough, it would be served at dinner. Jamie Oliver and Hugh Fearnley-Whittingstall were among the many young chefs given a chance here. This was a kitchen which developed its dishes from first principles, starting with ingredients, not technique. The food was expected to emanate the warmth and love of a Tuscan farmer's wife, not the austerity of a chef in a tall, white toque.

For Ruth Rogers and Rose Gray, success came in a supportive environment. They were already well-liked and well-known figures in London. Rogers's husband was working next door, running a thriving architectural practice whose employees and clients were their earliest customers. They still had to build a restaurant from scratch, to prove themselves as chefs and owners, to convert their love of Italian ingredients and cooking into an experience that people loved and were willing to pay for. But they were not operating against a void.

Halfway up Sweden, close to Norway, tucked in between mountains, forests and a skein of scraggly roads is one of the most quixotic and admired restaurants in the world. It is hard to imagine a less obvious place for an ambitious chef to pursue opportunity. But this is where Magnus Nilsson has chosen to make his stand, in a collection of farm buildings which now houses a hotel and restaurant called Fäviken. Its owner is a prominent fund manager in Stockholm, but it is Nilsson who is its innovator and public face.

Nilsson grew up not far away, in Östersund, the capital of Jämtland County, a town of fewer than 50,000 people huddled on the shore of an inland lake in the middle of Sweden's empty heart. His grandfather raised livestock and grew vegetables. As a boy, Nilsson learned to hunt and cook game. But from a young age, he wanted to get away, to somewhere with more people and more life. He apprenticed at his first restaurant at the age of fourteen, went away to cooking school at sixteen and by nineteen, he had reached Paris. He spent several years renting a tiny maid's room and experiencing the hierarchies and brutality of Paris's greatest restaurants. When he wasn't cooking, learning to caress vegetables in the pan and turn cold butter and flour into delicious pastry, he was eating, spending everything he earned

Rule-breakers do best in a supportive context.

on meals in the best restaurants he could afford. In his mid twenties, he returned to Sweden. But he could not find a place with the same regard for ingredients as he had found in Paris. And so, reluctantly, he stopped cooking and turned to wine.

As he worked towards his Master of Wine qualification, a friend invited him to build a cellar for the family which owned Fäviken. It would mean a return home, to the place where, he wrote, 'I promised myself I wouldn't waste any time working, as its inhabitants, I believed, were chronically uninterested in ambitious restaurants, and the vast bulk of its produce, as I remembered it, exceedingly uninspiring.'[4] At the time, Fäviken was used mostly for moose-fondue dinners for corporate groups, and Nilsson worked the front of house. But he was a different man now from the young chef who had left in his teens. He had a steady girlfriend, and as he lived on the estate and discovered its gardens, as he visited the neighbouring farms and began to hunt and fish again, he began to discern the possibilities for a restaurant which established its own standards. It would plunge its roots into the bleak landscape of Jämtland and see what grew. The owners and Nilsson established three criteria for a new restaurant: that it be economically sound and sustainable; of the highest quality; and source its produce as locally as possible.

The constraints of cooking with local produce in a region frozen for many months each year stimulated Nilsson's creativity. It forced him to think differently, to find a way to bring acid to a dish without lemons, to make something of the grouse brought to the kitchen door by a local hunter. He learned about pickling and canning, how to preserve what he grew from spring to autumn in a root cellar through the winter. He studied the local cows and discovered that former dairy cows offered more interesting meat than beef cattle. Over months and years, talented chefs started drifting north to work with him, signing up to a life in this curious place, and more customers began making the long trek, drawn to Nilsson's warm, wooden dining room with furs hanging by the stairs and cured meats dangling from the rafters. In a world chasing the rare experience, Fäviken provides just that.

Neither Rose Gray nor Magnus Nilsson followed a conventional route to the top of their profession. But they chose to work in a context which favoured them. Nilsson had struggled in the extreme formality and callous churn of Parisian restaurants. But he thrived in a place he had known since he was a boy. It is hard to imagine a French chef ever succeeding in Fäviken the way Nilsson has.

Any entrepreneur choosing where to do their work should think about context in similar terms. It's not about going where everyone else is going, where the contest will be fiercest and the rivalries intense. It is about going to the place where you will have a natural edge over every other sucker who rolls into town, where you can take the risk that others never could.

4. Planning

The designer Charles Eames said that with each of his designs, he spent 1 per cent of his energy conceiving it and 99 per cent holding on to that original conception throughout its implementation and fabrication. The writer Joan Didion found she had a very different problem in getting a project going. 'What's so hard about the first sentence is that you're stuck with it. Everything else is going to flow out of that sentence. And by the time you've laid down the first two sentences, your options are all gone.'

Right from the start of each project, Eames's greatest challenge was *how*, whereas Didion's was *what*. This is the difference between designing a building or a piece of furniture, which requires the use of materials, measurements and the opinions of others, and the solitary writer's work of putting pen to a blank sheet of paper. But both Eames and Didion were grappling with a similar problem, which was holding on to their room for manoeuvre as a project progressed and their options shut down. Figuring out the *how* even as they tried to home in and hold on to the *what*. For entrepreneurs, all strategic and tactical decision-making boils down to this central problem: building the plane at the same time as you hurtle towards take-off.

The German field marshal Helmuth von Moltke observed that 'no plan of operations survives first contact with the enemy', and it is rare for a business plan to survive contact with the market. But

Moltke didn't get to be Chief of the Prussian General Staff during Germany's Wars of Unification by showing up on the battlefield with a currywurst spilling down his jacket front and hoping to wing it. All he was saying was that plans need to adapt to circumstance. Strategy and tactics need to inform and reinforce each other continuously.

It used to be that to raise money for a business, an entrepreneur needed a business plan. Business schools built courses around the structure of the business plan, starting with the financials often projected several years into the future, a sales-and-marketing plan, research into the competition and so forth. These thirty-page documents would circulate amongst potential investors. But the real value of the business plan is not to secure investment. It is to help the entrepreneur to think through the business, to move from daydreaming to reality. The numbers in the plan don't need to be right, just considered inasmuch as they point to the likely levers and pressure points in the business. If you are planning a restaurant and you find that your desired location is going to gobble up an unseemly proportion of your budget, then you might consider another location, or a higher-margin form of food service. If you discover that the health-and-safety costs of your new construction business are always going to exceed the costs you can charge to customers, you might want to look at a less competitive field of building. The business plan should not be a vacuous marketing exercise intended to shill investors, or holy writ for the new company. But it can be an invaluable checkpoint for the rational entrepreneur. It allows you to think about what you might need before you actually need it.

One of the difficulties for entrepreneurs is that creating value for others and turning a profit for yourself may require contradictory thinking and actions. To create value you need to be wide open to the world, to absorb influences, straddle different fields and spy opportunity. You need to engage other people and persuade them to join you on your journey. You must be open to experimentation and feedback. To capture value for yourself requires control and discretion. You must be a canny negotiator, a manager of incentives, a fierce competitor, a minimizer of costs and maximizer of profits. You must obsess over details in the short term to guarantee success in the long term. The planner and the dreamer, the quartermaster and improviser must exist in the same person.

Every year, with its annual report, Amazon attaches a copy of a letter to shareholders written by the company's founder and CEO, Jeff Bezos, in 1997. The point is to show that for all the changes that have occurred at the company since, it has remained consistent in its fundamental approach to management and decision-making. The letter begins by stating that it is 'Day One for the Internet' and for Amazon. If all goes well, it will solidify its position in an increasingly crowded field of competitors. Its goal is market leadership, as whoever emerges as the market leader will benefit from the network effects of e-commerce and grow exponentially larger. It will focus on reporting cash flows rather than accounting gimmicks, and invest in the long term, in the technology infrastructure to guarantee a market-leading position. It will stay lean and cost-conscious, a policy embodied by the use of cheap wooden doors on sawhorses as desks. The letter was a progress report and a statement of intent. It is proof that for a start-up with the right balance of short- and long-term thinking, tactical nous and strategic planning, extraordinary success is achievable.

V. Exploiting Opportunity

1. The Struggle

By the end of 2008, Elon Musk was in terrible financial straits. He was thirty-seven years old and had already made close to $200 million as a Silicon Valley entrepreneur, most of it from the sale of the payments company PayPal to eBay. But he had plunged that fortune back into two new ventures, SpaceX and Tesla, one to send privately funded rockets into space, the other to build electric cars. Now, he was about to lose it all.

Musk is revered in the technology industry for his audacity and brilliance, but at that moment, it looked like his ambitions would sink him. To make matters worse, he was going through a very public divorce from the mother of his five children. 'I was just getting pistol-whipped,' he said.

> There was a lot of *Schadenfreude* at the time, and it was bad on so many levels . . . It hurt really bad. You have these huge doubts that your life is not working, your car is not working, you're going through a divorce and all of those things. I felt like a pile of shit. I didn't think we would overcome it. I thought things were probably fucking doomed.[1]

His then girlfriend and later second wife, Talulah Riley, would watch him reading his emails and grimacing. His weight went up and down and he looked exhausted. He suffered from nightmares and would wake up screaming, crawling up Riley's body. Friends lent him money, and employees at Tesla wrote cheques, not thinking they'd ever see the money again.

That December, as both Tesla and SpaceX were about to go bankrupt, Musk took money out of SpaceX and shuffled it into Tesla. He received $15 million when a company started by his cousins, in which he'd invested, was sold to Dell, and put that straight into his companies. He had to chivvy Tesla's existing investors to come up with more.

Yet in one extraordinary forty-eight-hour span before Christmas, he pulled it all around. Hours before he would have to miss the payroll at Tesla, his investors agreed to write him another cheque. Then word came from NASA that SpaceX had been selected as a supplier for the International Space Station, and would be paid $1.6 billion for twelve flights. Musk wept as the two deals came together. He compared his frenzied fundraising and deal-making to *The Matrix*, but astonishingly he had pulled it off.

An old friend of his said:

What he went through in 2008 would have broken anyone else. That ability to stay focussed in the midst of a crisis stands as one of Musk's main advantages over other executives and competitors. Most people who are under that sort of pressure fray. Their decisions go bad. Elon gets hyper-rational. He's still able to make very clear, long-term decisions. The harder it gets, the better he gets. Anyone who saw what he went through firsthand came away with more respect for the guy. I've just never seen anything like his ability to take pain.[2]

Ben Horowitz is one of the most successful investors in Silicon Valley. He has founded and run his own start-up and funded others. He believes that Karl Marx's observation that 'life is struggle' applies particularly to entrepreneurs. They all start their companies with dreams of hiring the best people and creating the best products, of improving the world. Then reality sets in. The product doesn't work. People turn out to be treacherous. Once-enthusiastic customers start to bail. The money runs out and they can't raise any more for reasons beyond their control. A run on Asian currencies crimps investing around the world. The landlord puts up the rent. 'As your dreams turn into nightmares, you find yourself in the Struggle,' Horowitz writes. The prospect of failure becomes all-consuming. You cannot sleep or take a holiday because being away from the business feels worse than working. You feel alone, no longer a person, just a bundle of obligations, surrounded by people who want, want, want, none of whom want to give. 'The Struggle is where your guts boil so much that you feel like you are going to spit blood . . . The Struggle is not failure, but it causes failure. Especially if you are weak. Always if you are weak. Most people are not strong enough.'[3]

Every form of entrepreneurship involves the Struggle. Once someone chooses a career as an artist, they are immediately faced with the challenge of making a living while nourishing that part of them which generates the art. Some will find their juices flowing at the thought of a pay cheque, while others will freeze and feel corrupted. And that is before they have even put brush to paper or finger to keyboard. The American sculptor Anne Truitt compared artists to riders hurtling time and again into the rain-swept night, with no sense of where they are heading.

If you think your Struggle's hard, try space exploration.

When they find that they have ridden and ridden – maybe for years, full tilt – in what is for them a mistaken direction, they must unearth within themselves some readiness to turn direction and to gallop off again. They may spend a little time scraping off the mud, resting the horse, having a hot bath, laughing and sitting in candlelight with friends. But in the back of their minds they never forget that the dark, driving run is theirs to make again. They need their balances in order to support their risks. The more they develop an understanding of all their experience – the more it is at their command – the more they carry with them into the whistling wind.[4]

It is only by saddling up time and again that you have the slightest chance of making the Struggle any easier.

2. Being and Becoming

However tough the Struggle, it is worth the entrepreneur recalling that many people are eager to be led, to follow a daring pioneer towards an exorbitant goal. Elon Musk may have come close to a nervous breakdown trying to sustain his various ventures, but for those who followed him into battle, the rewards came in all kinds of forms.

In order to recruit his first employees at SpaceX, Musk started at the best university aeronautics programmes in America. He asked about the students who had received the highest exam scores and called them in their dormitory rooms. He pitched them the idea of his private rocket company, saying that they would be building a rocket the moment they started work, not putting on a suit and tie and sitting behind a desk. Word soon spread to the major government contractors, firms like Boeing and Lockheed Martin, where a rocket scientist could languish for years, filling out forms instead of playing with machinery. The jobs at those industrial giants were comfortable but futile. At SpaceX, Musk told his engineers to buy themselves a chair at Staples, go shopping at a nearby electronics parts superstore and get to work. The engineers would work all day and night, load their generators and rockets into the backs of pickup trucks and drive them from Los Angeles out into the Mojave Desert to test them.

The intensity and camaraderie of the work became addictive. When the company found a viable test site in the middle of Texas, some 1,400 miles from the SpaceX factory in California, teams of engineers would load their equipment into a U-Haul trailer, hitch it to the back of a Hummer and drive back and forth across the country. Their engines would frequently explode, in what came to be known as 'rapid unscheduled disassemblies'. But under pressure from Musk and with his encouragement to be as creative as they knew how, to fix problems rather than bunker down in their established disciplines, the engineers soon developed ways of experimenting at rates inconceivable at a much larger company. Soon, they could build an engine in just three days. When necessary, Musk himself would spend all night at his factory with his engineers, his designer clothes and shoes covered in machine gunk.

In 2007, SpaceX began shipping people and equipment out to Kwajalein Island, a speck of land in the Marshall Islands in the Pacific Ocean, which had served for years as a base for the US military to test its longest-range missiles and 'Star Wars' space-weapons programme. Here in oppressive, tropical heat, the engineers set up camp. They would work from dawn till dusk preparing to launch their first rocket, and eat as a group in the evenings. During their off hours, some fished, others learned to dive, and they all shared their expert knowledge of their very different fields of rocket science. It was a rocket-building adventure out of an adolescent's dreams.

The results were far from perfect. At the first launch in March 2006, the Falcon 1 fell to earth twenty-five seconds into flight. The following spring, it lasted five minutes before breaking apart. It would be two more years, and many millions of dollars of Musk's personal fortune later, before SpaceX had its first successful flight. But the reason those engineers stuck around, when they could have taken better paid, less arduous jobs elsewhere, was that Musk was leading them on a mission, one that made their lives and work worthwhile. After that first failed launch, Musk wrote in a letter to his employees: 'A friend of mine wrote to remind me that only 5 of the first 9 Pegasus launches succeeded; 3 of 5 for Ariane; 9 of 20 for Atlas; 9 of 21 for Soyuz; and 9 of 18 for Proton. Having experienced firsthand how hard it is to reach orbit, I have a lot of respect for those that persevered to produce the vehicles that are mainstays of space launch today.' SpaceX, he concluded, 'is in this for the long haul and, come hell or high water, we are going to make this work.'[5]

Entrepreneurship pursued in this way offers both the entrepreneur and those along for the ride the opportunity to do more than just deal with obstacles. They cease to be pragmatists and become vitalists, people who seek to become through their work more than they were before. Their work gives them the opportunity to display heroic virtues of determination, courage and cunning. It is the difficulty of entrepreneurship that leads to the fullest imaginable life. Work provides the framework for self-discovery, for finding out who we can be when we meet great challenges. And this is often more than who we are when we fill out expense forms and refill the coffee maker.

3. Failure 1 and Failure 2

In the thick of all this talk of daring, risk and struggle lurks the problem of failure. Failures exist along a very broad spectrum, and all too often the many kinds of failures are confused in the minds of those wishing to think like entrepreneurs. Often, you will hear successful entrepreneurs talking about the many failures which littered the path to their eventual glory. But they are not all talking about the same kind of failure. There are relatively trivial failures, like failing to meet a product deadline or giving a duff speech at a conference. And then there are the soul-shaking failures, those all-consuming failures of self which can force even the doughtiest entrepreneurs to their knees. It is useful to think of these failures in two broad categories, Failure 1 and Failure 2, and then consider which you want more of and which you would do everything to avoid.

Failure 1 includes the failures intrinsic to the scientific method. You come up with a hypothesis and then test it. Most of the time, your test will not support your hypothesis. In that sense it is a failure. But in the sense that it has eliminated a possibility and allowed you to narrow down the field of possible proofs, then it has been a success. This is the kind of failure Thomas Edison was thinking about when he said, 'I have not failed. I've just found 10,000 ways that won't work.'

Francis Crick said that he and James Watson discovered the structure of DNA because of their 'willingness to discard ideas when they became untenable'. They did not cling to the old for the sake of it. They kept building physical models of the possible structures and tinkering with them, just like Elon Musk's rocket scientists, faster than the competition in order to get to a structure that made sense. 'Most attempts fail not because of lack of brains but because the investigator gets stuck in a cul-de-sac or gives up too soon,' wrote Crick.[6] Rapid experimentation and the many failures that entails led to their eventual triumph.

Within the priesthood of software developers, a small book with a rough brown cover showing a wilting leaf is passed around with reverence. *Wabi-Sabi for Artists, Designers, Poets & Philosophers* is coveted because of what it says about creativity. The Japanese concept of 'Wabi-sabi', it begins, 'is a beauty of things imperfect, imperman-ent and incomplete. It is a beauty of things modest and humble. It is a beauty of things unconventional.'[7]

It used to be that when starting a company, you needed a product, something fully formed and marketable. Nowadays, with customers more willing to be part of the product-development process, you may be better off with a prototype, a Beta version which you can ship and test repeatedly with your potential market. Google's Gmail service stayed in Beta for five years after its launch, from 2004 to 2009. Even as millions of people used it, it remained publicly and internally a work in progress. Imperfect. Incomplete. Impermanent.

Wabi-Sabi does not focus on the creator but rather on the object: the beautiful, unsigned pot, the product of centuries of pot-making craft. Similarly, the code underlying a software company is the cre-ation of many people, their individual traces all but invisible in the end product. The code itself is never perfect. It is imperfect from the moment of its creation, and will have to be repeatedly updated and rewritten. Its imperfection is not a reflection of failure, but a form of beauty in itself.

At Facebook, slogans have been painted on the walls to inspire employees: 'Move fast, and break things!'; 'Done is better than perfect!'; 'What would you do if you were not afraid?' It is unlikely that a world-class chef would have similar slogans on the walls of his restaurant. But software and haute cuisine require very different kinds of entrepreneurial approach.

Failure 1 includes the repeated failures and rejections inherent in selling. Every good salesperson knows her odds. Will it take ten calls to get a sale or a hundred? She knows how to learn and improve from every rejection and never to take it personally.

Also in this category of Failure 1 are failures of the privileged. Failing to get a job, failing to raise money for your start-up, failing to get promoted at work, failing to win political office. These are merely speed bumps in any life, moments perhaps for self-reflection. But for anyone to depict them as more reveals a shallowness of experience.

Failure 2 is the kind of failure that tests you as a person. It is the kind of failure Nietzsche had in mind when he said 'that which does not destroy me, makes me stronger'. These are the failures which dance you along the abyss. These include failures of addiction, of criminal behaviour which endangers the lives and livelihoods of others, of losing everything you have and everything your friends and family have invested in you. The kind of failure which jolted Elon Musk from sleep. The alternative to coming back stronger, in Nietzsche's formulation, is destruction. Arthur Miller's Willy Loman killed himself at the end of *Death of a Salesman*, ruined by his failure as a husband, father and businessman. He simply failed, failed and then ended it all. Failure destroyed him. These are the risks of Failure 2, the kind you don't mess around with. You don't court this failure in the hope of a teachable moment. You run from it and minimize its menace. Only if you have to, do you search through its melancholy consequences for sources of new growth.

4. Indifference and Lightness

The struggles of entrepreneurship and the fear of soul-shattering failure have turned many entrepreneurs to philosophies of indifference, notably Stoicism and Zen. The Stoics recommended we contemplate the worst possible experiences in life, such as the death of a child, in order to immunize ourselves emotionally to suffering. If we spent enough time imagining the worst, it could never take us by surprise. If we practised sleeping in the streets in a rough cloak, we could act without fear of losing what we have and thus make better, less emotional, decisions. The most famous Stoic of all, Seneca, achieved great worldly success as a businessman and advisor to the Emperor Nero. But he was also exiled for committing adultery with the sister of the Emperor Caligula and eventually ordered by Nero to commit suicide. If he practised what he preached, and there is scepticism among historians that he did, neither his ups nor his downs would have much bothered him. Zen, crudely understood, offers a similar kind of emotional therapy, forcing us out of our worries about the past and future, about pain and suffering, to focus intently on the present.

For six months in the winter of 2009–2010, I travelled back and forth from New York to Cupertino, California, to work on a new project at Apple. Steve Jobs was desperately ill at the time and concerned with what would happen to the company after his death.

He had decided to establish Apple University, an internal leadership programme, and my assignment was to consider what made Apple Apple and draft some ideas for how to teach that to Apple's busy managers. My office consisted of a desk in a stationery closet down the corridor from the absent Jobs and his then Chief Operating Officer, Tim Cook.

Trying to understand Apple felt at first like trying to climb a sheer glass wall. There were none of the usual handholds. Apple does not publish a glossy annual report, beyond its raw 10K filing to the Securities and Exchange Commission. The executives, I was told, were not going to have a lot of time to discuss their work, let alone abstractions such as the Appleness of Apple. To understand its business and economics, you had to begin from the outside and work your way in.

What quickly became apparent was that Jobs's goal of disentangling himself from his company was going to be difficult. His character defined Apple. He was an entrepreneurial one-off. You could try to elicit lessons from his behaviour, but they would be difficult for anyone besides him to apply. For instance, he would park his silver Mercedes SL 55 AMG in a disabled spot close to the entrance of Apple's headquarters at One Infinite Loop. The car had no licence plates, as he leased a new one every six months, and California gave you six months to get plates for a new car. Were these the behaviours of a blithe genius, indifferent to the rules which bound ordinary mortals? Or a jerk?

His internal architecture was unique, the source of the intuitions and attitudes which led him to create Apple in the first place, and then recreate it in 1997 when it was near bankruptcy and he returned as its CEO. He would toss out koans which everyone around him then struggled to dissect: Apple's work was at the crossroads of liberal arts and technology; what you say 'no' to is as important as what you say 'yes' to; good design makes the complex simple. Managers might gobble up anything with Steve Jobs's name attached, but these ideas were far more nuanced than, say, the importance of cash flow versus earnings. To explain them in a way that separated them from Jobs's own personality and experiences was a challenge.

One evening, part desperate and part curious about Jobs's fascination with Zen Buddhism, I went to the Kannon Do Zen Meditation Center in Mountain View, a barnlike meditation room filled with men and women of every age, most working for technology businesses. We were told to sit cross-legged on a low cushion facing a bare white wall for forty-five minutes. As each thought or worry entered our mind, we were advised to let it go, to let it waft away like a balloon, because for now there was nothing to be done. And so I did, wondering at first what Steve Jobs saw in all this, then eventually wondering about nothing at all.

I realized afterwards that to be so focussed on the present and future, as Jobs was, is most unusual. For such people, the past is constantly cast aside. It does not matter. The old ties, old models, are irrelevant. It can seem cruel and unfeeling. But it makes for a great entrepreneur.

Jobs knew better than anyone the fragility of business success. He had been the most famous entrepreneur in the world in his early twenties, and then fired from his own company at thirty. But he had come back. Building a business, he would say, was not for the mentally sane. It was for the passionate and maddeningly persistent.

The closest he had ever come to articulating a personal philosophy was in a commencement speech at Stanford in 2005, the definitive entrepreneurial text of our age. He offered up three lessons in that speech, closely linked to his long fascination with Zen. The first was to trust your gut. Too much planning rules out serendipity. As a student he had dropped into a college calligraphy class, and years later this led to the variety of fonts on the first Apple Macintosh. All the random choices you make in life only ever make sense when you glance back and connect the dots.

The second was to value loss. He had been fired from Apple when he was thirty. It seemed devastating at the time, but opened the way for him to create two more companies, Pixar, the animation studio, and NeXT, which was eventually bought by Apple. Loss gave him the time to recognize what he loved in life: his work and his family.

The third lesson was about living in the face of death. He had been diagnosed with pancreatic cancer a year before and was given just a few months to live. Death, he said, was life's 'change agent' as it 'clears out the old to make way for the new'. The inevitability of death gives us no time to do anything but trust our 'inner voice'.

Each was a powerful lesson, deceptively simple, yet requiring great discipline and strength of character to follow.

One afternoon in the autumn of 1969, the Irish playwright Samuel Beckett was staying at a hotel in Tunisia when the telephone rang. His French wife, Suzanne, answered. She turned to Beckett and said '*Quelle catastrophe!*' He had been awarded the Nobel Prize in Literature. Scrutiny would follow. Requests for interviews. Photographers would soon be descending on their hotel, forcing Beckett to scurry out through a service entrance to go for a swim. His precious solitude would be compromised.

For years, Beckett had fought for and guarded his freedom as a writer. Long after he achieved great success, he continued to live in the same small, austere apartment in Paris. His study was sparsely furnished with a desk and chair, and overlooked the courtyard of the Santé prison. Beckett had long been fascinated by prisons, by justice and injustice, imprisonment and freedom; by the brevity of existence and the primacy of our interior lives over the random judgements of society. The howls of the prisoners were the soundtrack to his work.

The conditions Beckett created for himself were consistent with much else in his life. To think, he went on long, solitary walks, often during the night. As a young man, he abandoned a promising career in academia to write. While he figured out what to write, he lived drunkenly and listlessly in Paris, often broke, and served as a courier for the French Resistance during World War II. But once the war ended, as he turned forty, he realized his purpose. It was not to be in trying to mimic his literary hero and friend, James Joyce, by adding ever more layers of complexity to his writing. It was to be through 'impoverishment, in lack of knowledge and in taking away, in subtracting rather than in adding'. He would strip his work of style, of narrative, plot, all the standard writerly tools. He would plunder his inner world, not try to describe the world he saw around him. And so began what he called 'the siege in the room', the years of intense productivity which built his reputation.

Even as Beckett became famous, as his plays were performed all over the world, he continued to resist the accretion of acclaim. He had to try harder than ever to have less. In 1958, before the first American production of his play *Endgame*, he wrote to the American director Alan Schneider: 'Success and failure on the public level never mattered much to me, in fact I feel much more at home with the latter, having breathed deep of its vivifying air all my writing life up to the last couple of years.'[8]

He considered rejecting the Nobel Prize as his friend Jean-Paul Sartre had done, as he felt like a tombstone was being placed on his writing career. But he didn't want to appear to be copying Sartre. So he asked his editor Jérôme Lindon to travel to Stockholm to receive the prize, and a publisher friend to send him a list of writers who could use financial help. He then set about disbursing his £30,000 in prize money. He sent $3,000 to his old friend Djuna Barnes, who was living in penury in New York. The novelist B. S. Johnson bought a sports car with his gift. Beckett had received the Nobel in the course of a telephone call, and rid himself of it almost as quickly.

There is a wonderful paparazzo photograph taken of him in 1978 showing him strolling through the streets of Tangier in shorts, sandals and an open-necked shirt. He is wearing sunglasses and carrying a small bag over his shoulder on his way to the beach. He looks entirely carefree. His rejection of the encumbrances of literary fame had clearly worked.

On the spectrum of human achievement, Steve Jobs and Samuel Beckett might seem poles apart. Jobs the prototypical entrepreneur. Beckett the brooding intellectual. Jobs the organization builder and billionaire. Beckett the solitary genius and ascetic. But in significant ways, they thought along similar lines. They met success while hiking along unconventional paths, Beckett after years of dissolute squalor in Paris, Jobs when thrust to the boundaries of the Silicon Valley world he once ruled. They found their purpose not by trying to make sense of the world, but first by making sense of themselves.

The rewards of their work scarcely seemed to matter compared to the work itself. The world frequently sought to smother them in acclaim or disdain, but they battled both extremes to protect their lightness of being, their freedom of manoeuvre, their right to stroll unharried to a day at the beach, to drive without plates and park where they damned well liked.

Both lived as Beckett put it 'astride of a grave', conscious that 'the light gleams an instant, then it's night once more'.[9]

To think like an entrepreneur is not just to draw up a spreadsheet. It is not just to mess around with a product, to create a website, invest in some Google AdWords and hope for the best. It is to think in terms of change, often dramatic change. And to change anything, one must move lightly, unburdened by the drab expectations of others.

Homework

There are many resources for entrepreneurs, books, films and websites which can help you with everything from thinking through psychological, personal and business risk to new means of product development and achieving a great exit. I'd recommend the following in each section as a place to start.

I. The Entrepreneurial Mind

Luke Johnson's *Start It Up: Why Running Your Own Business is Easier Than You Think* is brilliantly readable and encouraging. Johnson is a successful entrepreneur himself and a lively and empathetic writer.

The documentary film *Hearts of Darkness: A Filmmaker's Apocalypse* tells the story of the filming of *Apocalypse Now*, mostly from the perspective of Eleanor Coppola, the wife of the director, Francis Ford Coppola. It is a blistering account of the minefield of entrepreneurial creativity and execution. Coppola's empathy for entrepreneurs is also beautifully expressed in his film *Tucker: The Man and his Dream*. For more on Frank Gehry, I'd recommend Sydney Pollack's documentary *Sketches of Frank Gehry*.

John Paul Getty's *How to be Rich* is a collection of his essays for *Playboy*. Getty is clear-eyed and uncompromising. The choice to pursue great business success and great riches often requires one to live at odds with society. It demands choices and compromises.

Of Richard Branson's several books, the best is his autobiography, *Losing My Virginity: How I Survived, Had Fun and Made a Fortune Doing Business My Way.*

Roger Lowenstein's biography of Warren Buffett, *Buffett: The Making of an American Capitalist*, is an exemplary work of business history and biography which explains the thinking of arguably the most successful investor in history. Buffett's behaviours run consistently throughout his business and personal life, with frugality, a sense of value and force of habit all playing dominant roles.

Influence: The Psychology of Persuasion by Robert Cialdini is an essential work for selling, hiring and managing.

Emerson's essay *Self-Reliance* is thorny and challenging, and may be the best thing you can read on the thinking of Steve Jobs, who adored it. The best business account of Jobs is not about Apple, but about Pixar, his animation company. *The Pixar Touch* by David A. Price explains how great opportunities often take time and brilliant teams to evolve, not just a single great mind.

Meg Cadoux Hirshberg's *For Better or for Work*, about being married to an entrepreneur, Gary Hirshberg, the founder of Stonyfield Farm, is excellent on the toll your choice to be an entrepreneur will take on those closest to you.

Investing in a weekend of Start-Up Weekend is a useful immersion into modern start-up culture. Over fifty-four intense hours, you will form a team, with friends or strangers, and learn how to create a company and pitch it. Entrepreneurship needn't be at all like the Start-Up Weekend experience, but you may learn something about yourself and how other aspiring entrepreneurs think in this concentrated setting.

II. A Brief History of an Idea

Peter Drucker's *Innovation and Entrepreneurship* gives a thorough theoretical and practical grounding in the history of entrepreneurship and its links to innovation.

Martha Lane Fox's blog, marthalanefoxblog.wordpress.com, contains rich insights from both an entrepreneurial and policymaking perspective on technology, entrepreneurship and their links to a more open, civilized society.

III. Searching for Opportunity

Steven Johnson's *Where Good Ideas Come From: The Natural History of Innovation* provides a historical perspective on the evolution of ideas. Even the most egocentric entrepreneurs must admit that they stand on the shoulders of others.

Twyla Tharp's *The Creative Habit: Learn It and Use It for Life* describes how a choreographer searches for new ideas. She has a set of processes which any aspiring entrepreneur might find helpful.

Creative Confidence by David and Tom Kelley, the co-founders of the product-design company IDEO, offers a similar process-driven approach to finding and developing new ideas.

IV. Responding to Opportunity

Silicon Valley's community of investors and bloggers provides fertile ground for thinking about entrepreneurship. The material at the Venture Hacks blog, www.venturehacks.com, is occasional but always excellent for anyone considering a technology start-up. And from there, it is worth scouring the activity on its partner site Angel List, https://angel.co, to see what's getting funded.

Ben Horowitz is a partner at the venture-capital firm Andreessen Horowitz and his blog, bhorowitz.com, and book, *The Hard Thing about Hard Things*, offer sensational insight into the realities of setting up a business and running it through positive and negative cycles. He will make you feel less of a fool when things go wrong. If you're inspired by rap lyrics, Horowitz offers plenty of those.

The most influential CEO in Silicon Valley's history is Andy Grove of Intel and his book *Only the Paranoid Survive* is essential reading. After you have finished it, you can never say anyone told you it would be easy. Michael Bloomberg's *Bloomberg by Bloomberg* is equally punchy and honest. For a very different kind of entrepreneurial profile, a favourite is Alexandra Jacobs on Sara Blakeley, the founder of Spanx, in the *New Yorker*, 28 March 2011.

VI. Exploiting Opportunity

Grinding It Out, Ray Kroc's story of building McDonald's, is a fascinating dissection of the importance of choosing the right business model and executing relentlessly to make it work. Similarly, Sam

Walton's *Made in America*. Even if you don't like McDonald's or Walmart, Kroc's and Walton's ways of thinking and executing are highly instructive.

Peter Thiel's *Zero to One: Notes on Startups*, or *How to Build the Future*, is bursting with provocative theories which may only make sense if you live in Palo Alto, California. But it is easy to read and will sharpen any entrepreneurial mind.

Notes

Introduction

1 'Want to Start a Startup?' Paul Graham, Y Combinator, August 2007.
2 Daniel Kahneman, *Thinking, Fast and Slow* (London: Penguin, 2012), pp. 257–63.
3 Ibid, p. 256.
4 Mark Halperin and John Heilemann, *Game Change* (London: Harper, 2010), p. 60.
5 Ibid, p. 73.
6 Edmund Phelps, *Mass Flourishing: How Grassroots Innovation Created Jobs, Challenge, and Change* (New York: Knopf, 2013), p. ix.

I. The Entrepreneurial Mind

1 George Gurdjieff, *Meetings with Remarkable Men* (London: Penguin, 1997).
2 For a comprehensive account of this nonsense: 'The Psyche of the Entrepreneur', Daniel Goleman, *New York Times*, 2 February 1986.
3 J. Rogers Hollingsworth, 'High Cognitive Complexity and the Making of Major Scientific Discoveries', in A. Sales & M. Fournier (eds), *Knowledge, Communication and Creativity* (London: SAGE Publications Ltd, 2007), pp. 129–56.
4 E. O. Wilson, *Naturalist* (Washington DC: Island Press, 2006).
5 E. O. Wilson, *Consilience: The Unity of Knowledge* (London: Abacus, 1999).
6 J. Rogers Hollingsworth, 'High Cognitive Complexity and the Making of Major Scientific Discoveries', in A. Sales & M. Fournier (eds), *Knowledge, Communication and Creativity* (London: SAGE Publications Ltd, 2007).

7 Todd Bishop, *GeekWire*, 27 October 2011. 'Gates to students: Don't try to be a billionaire, it's overrated.'

8 Jacob Bernstein, 'Givenchy's Riccardo Tisci is the King of Fashion Week', *New York Times*, 16 September 2015.

9 Ibid.

10 Garage Technology Ventures presents Silicon Valley 4.0., 7 October 2003.

11 Dane Stangler, *The Age of the Entrepreneur: Demographics and Entrepreneurship* (Kauffman Foundation, 2013).

12 Paul Goldberger, 'Why Frank Gehry is not a "Starchitect"', *Vanity Fair*, September 2015.

13 Matt Tyrnauer, 'Architecture in the Age of Gehry', *Vanity Fair*, August 2010.

14 Paul Goldberger, 'Why Frank Gehry is not a "Starchitect"', *Vanity Fair*, September 2015.

15 Edward Lazear, James Liang and Hui Wang, 'Demographics and Entrepreneurship', NBER working paper 20506, September 2014.

16 This story and what follows is told by Steven Levy in his book *In the Plex* (London: Simon & Schuster, 2011).

II. A Brief History of an Idea

1 Joseph Schumpeter, *Capitalism, Socialism and Democracy* (first published 1942; new edition: London: Routledge, 2010), p. 132.

2 *Still Red Hot*, Rainey Kelly Campbell Roalfe / Y&R.

3 Peter Drucker, *Innovation and Entrepreneurship: Practice and Principles* (Harper & Row, 1985).

III. Searching for Opportunity

1 Amar Bhide, 'How Entrepreneurs Craft Strategies That Work', *Harvard Business Review*, March–April 1994.

2 Steven Johnson, 'The Genius of the Tinkerer', *Wall Street Journal*, 25 September 2010.

3 Francis Crick, *What Mad Pursuit* (London: Basic Books, 1998), pp. 15–18.

4   Bill Walsh, *The Score Takes Care of Itself: My Philosophy of Leadership* (London: Penguin, 2009), p. 44.

5   Clay Christensen developed the theory of disruption in his two books *The Innovator's Dilemma* (1997) and *The Innovator's Solution* (2003).

6   Clark Gilbert, 'The Disruption Opportunity', *MIT Sloan Management Review*, July 2003.

7   Steven Johnson, *How We Got to Now* (New York: Riverhead, 2014), p. 72.

IV. Responding to Opportunity

1   Jason Gissing, 'What my Goldman Sachs training taught me about entrepreneurship', *Financial Times*, 31 March 2015.

2   Ian Parker, 'The Shape of Things to Come', *New Yorker*, 23 February 2015.

3   Ronan Bennett, Rose Gray obituary, *Guardian*, 28 February 2010.

4   Magnus Nilsson, *Fäviken* (London: Phaidon, 2012).

V. Exploiting Opportunity

1   This quote and story are told on pp. 205–211 of *Elon Musk* by Ashlee Vance (London: Virgin Books, 2015).

2   Ibid.

3   Ben Horowitz, *The Hard Thing about Hard Things* (London: HarperBusiness, 2004), p. 61.

4   Anne Truitt, *Daybook* (New York: Scribner, 2013), p. 26.

5   This story is told in the chapter 'Mice in Space', in Ashlee Vance's biography of Musk, *Elon Musk* (London: Virgin Books, 2015).

6   Francis Crick, *What Mad Pursuit* (London: Basic Books, 1998), p. 74.

7   Leonard Koren, Introduction from *Wabi-Sabi for Artists, Designers, Poets & Philosophers* (Point Reyes, CA: Imperfect Publishing, 1994).

8   Robert Brustein, 'I Can't Go On, Alan. I'll Go On', *New York Times*, 31 January 1999.

9   Samuel Beckett, *Waiting for Godot* (first published 1954; new edition: London: Faber & Faber, 2012), II.

Acknowledgements

Many thanks to Dane Stangler, Wendy Guillies, Robert Litan, Nick Seguin and Carl Schramm, colleagues past and present at the Kauffman Foundation. To Alec Russell, Ravi Mattu and Adam Jones at the *Financial Times*. To Morgwn Rimel at The School of Life and to Cindy Chan and Robin Harvie at Macmillan. To the mighty Bo Fishback, physical and intellectual giant, tireless inspiration and all-round wizard on things entrepreneurial. And as ever to Margret, Augie and Hugo.

Picture Acknowledgements

The author and publisher would like to thank the following for permission to reproduce the images used in this book:

Pages 4–5 Red Dog Bar in Hoxton Square, London. Photo by Pawel Libera / LightRocket via Getty Images

Pages 10–11 President Barack Obama reads a document © Mary Evans / Everett Collection

Pages 14–15 Votes for Women Meeting in Hyde Park, June 1908 (b/w photo) / Hyde Park Corner, London, UK / © Mirrorpix / Bridgeman Images

Page 20 George Gurdjieff (b/w photo), French Photographer (20th century) / Private Collection / Archives Charmet / Bridgeman Images

Pages 24–5 Germany, accounting machine, typewriter. Photo by Fotografisches Atelier Ullstein / ullstein bild via Getty Images

Page 30 1950s boy Huck Finn style on homemade raft © Mary Evans / Classicstock / D. CORSON

Pages 44–5 Gar Pike and Common Pike fish © Mary Evans Picture Library

Page 52 Portrait of Nikola Tesla, 1890 (photo), Sarony, Napoleon (1821–96) / Private Collection / Prismatic Pictures / Bridgeman Images

Pages 60–1 Walden Pond in Lexington, Boston, USA (photo) /
  AA World Travel Library / Bridgeman Images
Page 73 Gillette safety razor blades. Photo by SSPL / Getty Images
Pages 102–3 Chefs Rose Gray and Ruth Rogers. Photo by Maurice
  ROUGEMONT / Gamma-Rapho via Getty Images
Pages 116–17 International Space Station / Encyclopaedia Britannica
  / UIG / Bridgeman Images

Notes

Notes

Notes

TOOLS FOR THINKING

A RANGE OF THOUGHTFUL STATIONERY, GAMES
& GIFTS FROM THE SCHOOL OF LIFE

Good thinking requires good tools. To complement our classes, books and therapies, THE SCHOOL OF LIFE now offers a range of stationery, games and gifts that are both highly useful and stimulating for the eye and mind.

THESCHOOLOFLIFE.COM

If you enjoyed this book, we'd encourage you to check out
other titles in the series:

Also Available:

If you'd like to explore more good ideas from everyday life,
THE SCHOOL OF LIFE runs a regular programme of classes, workshops,
and special events in London and other cities around the world.